I0455448

November 2013

NAVY SHIPBUILDING

Opportunities Exist to Improve Practices Affecting Quality

NAVY SHIPBUILDING

Opportunities Exist to Improve Practices Affecting Quality

GAO Highlights

Highlights of GAO-14-122, a report to congressional committees

Why GAO Did This Study

The Navy expects to spend about $15 billion per year to provide its fleet with the most advanced ships to support national defense and military strategies. Problems with recently delivered ships have focused attention on quality issues.

House Report No. 112-110, accompanying the Department of Defense Appropriations Bill, 2012, mandated that GAO review the Navy's quality assurance processes for new ship construction. This report discusses, among other issues, (1) quality problems in constructing recently delivered ships and Navy actions to improve quality and (2) key practices employed by leading commercial ship buyers and shipbuilders to ensure quality and how these compared with Navy practices.

GAO analyzed Navy data on ship quality from 2006 to May 2013 and spoke with Navy officials and shipbuilders. GAO also reviewed deficiency data for commercial ships and spoke with buyers and builders.

What GAO Recommends

To improve the construction quality of ships delivered to the Navy, GAO is recommending, among other things, that the Navy clarify policy on when deficiencies should be addressed, provide guidance on contract quality requirements, and assess applicability of certain commercial practices to Navy shipbuilding. DOD agreed with two recommendations and partially agreed with three, stating for example that current policy is adequate but that the Navy would monitor deficiency trends. GAO believes that the recommendations remain valid as discussed in the report.

View GAO-14-122. For more information, contact Michele Mackin at (202) 512-4841 or mackinm@gao.gov.

What GAO Found

The Navy has experienced significant quality problems with several ship classes over the past several years. It has focused on reducing the number of serious deficiencies at the time of delivery, and GAO's analysis shows that the number of deficiencies—particularly "starred" deficiencies designated as the most serious for operational or safety reasons—has generally dropped. Nonetheless, the Navy continues to accept ships with large numbers of open deficiencies (see figure below as an example; although total deficiencies have declined for this ship class, the last ship still had about 1,000 deficiencies that the shipbuilder was responsible for correcting). Accepting ships with large numbers of uncorrected deficiencies is a standard practice and GAO found that there are varying interpretations of Navy policy with regard to when the defects should be resolved. In 2009, the Navy organization that oversees ship construction launched the Back to Basics initiative to improve Navy oversight of ship construction. However, a key output of the initiative promoting consistent and adequate quality requirements in Navy contracts has yet to be implemented.

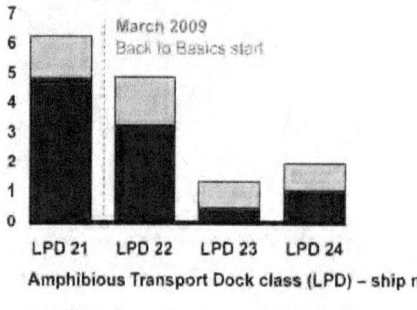

Deficiencies at Time of Delivery for LPD 17 Ship Class
Deficiencies (in thousands)

Amphibious Transport Dock class (LPD) – ship number

☐ Government   ■ Contractor

Source: GAO analysis of Navy data

Although the environment in which leading commercial ship buyers and builders operate differs in many ways from the Navy's, some commercial practices aimed at helping to ensure that ships are delivered with a minimum number of deficiencies may be informative for the Navy. Throughout the course of commercial shipbuilding projects, significant numbers of quality defects and instances of non-conforming work are identified. However, leading commercial ship buyers and shipbuilders make great efforts to ensure that these issues are resolved prior to delivery. Further, commercial ship buyers establish clear lines of accountability and hold their personnel responsible for ensuring the shipbuilder delivers a quality vessel. While commercial ship buyers focus on regularly witnessing in-process work through roaming patrols and impromptu inspections, Navy processes at the shipyards place less emphasis on in-process work. Moreover, leading commercial shipbuilders have strong quality management processes that track quality problems to the worker or supervisor level. Navy shipbuilding contractors have historically experienced difficulties in holding production workers and supervisors accountable for their work, but some of the shipyards reported they are making progress on increasing worker accountability.

_____ **United States Government Accountability Office**

Contents

Tables

Figures

Abbreviations

ABS	American Bureau of Shipping
DOD	Department of Defense
FPSO	Floating Production, Storage and Offloading vessel
INSURV	U.S. Navy Board of Inspection and Survey
LCS	Littoral Combat Ship
NAVSEA	Naval Sea Systems Command
NAVSEA 02	Naval Sea Systems Command Contracting Directorate
NAVSEA 04	Naval Sea Systems Command Logistics, Maintenance & Industrial Operations Directorate
NAVSEA 04Z	Naval Sea Systems Command Logistics, Maintenance & Industrial Operations Directorate, SUPSHIP Management Group
NAVSEA 05	Naval Sea Systems Command Engineering Directorate
NAVSEA 07	Naval Sea Systems Command Undersea Warfare Directorate
NAVSEA 08	Naval Sea Systems Command Nuclear Propulsion Directorate
NAVSEA 21	Naval Sea Systems Command Surface Warfare Directorate
PEO	U.S. Navy Program Executive Office
SUPSHIP	Naval Sea Systems Command Supervisor of Shipbuilding, Conversion and Repair
TSM	Technical Support Management data system

GAO U.S. GOVERNMENT ACCOUNTABILITY OFFICE

441 G St. N.W.
Washington, DC 20548

November 19, 2013

Congressional Committees

The Navy seeks to provide its fleet with the most advanced ships to support national defense and military strategies, expecting to spend about $15 billion per year building ships. Given the difficult operating environments and extended deployments for Navy ships, it is essential that they operate as expected. Yet several cases of poor quality in Navy shipbuilding programs have focused attention on quality issues for newly constructed ships. Many of the problems were attributed to issues with basic elements of shipbuilding, such as welding, installation of key systems (like propulsion and anchoring systems), and electrical work. The impact of poor quality can directly affect operational missions; for example, the first ship built in the USS *San Antonio* class (LPD 17) had to undergo emergency repairs during its first deployment that were primarily attributed to poor workmanship and a lack of quality control during the ship's construction. Recognizing that quality problems in shipbuilding needed to be addressed, the Navy established the "Back to Basics" initiative in 2009 to ensure the efficiency and quality of ship construction. The initiative focused on the Navy's Supervisor of Shipbuilding, Conversion and Repair (SUPSHIP)—the organization responsible for overseeing ship construction processes—and involved senior Naval Sea Systems Command leadership and the Navy Program Executive Offices responsible for managing the development and procurement of ships.

Also in 2009, we identified best practices from the commercial shipbuilding industry and made several recommendations to the Department of Defense to improve management of shipbuilding programs involving, among other things, knowledge needed at key decision points.[1] Building on that review, House Report No. 112-110, accompanying the Department of Defense Appropriations Bill, 2012 (H.R. 2219), mandated that we review the Navy's quality assurance processes for new ship construction. This report assesses (1) the extent to which newly constructed ships delivered to the Navy from 2006 through May 2013 had quality problems and the actions the Navy has taken to improve quality;

---

[1]See GAO, *Best Practices: High Levels of Knowledge at Key Points Differentiate Commercial Shipbuilding from Navy Shipbuilding*, GAO-09-322 (Washington, D.C.: May 13, 2009).

(2) key practices employed by leading commercial ship buyers and shipbuilders to ensure satisfactory quality and the extent to which Navy shipbuilding programs employ these practices; and (3) the role of classification societies (e.g., the American Bureau of Shipping) in Navy and commercial shipbuilding.

To identify the extent to which newly constructed Navy ships had quality problems and the actions the Navy has taken to improve quality, we reviewed Navy inspection reports, internal Navy reviews with regards to ship quality, ship delivery reports, shipbuilding contracts, and other documents discussing the quality of ships delivered to the Navy from 2006 through May 2013. We reviewed data on all ships delivered during this period but only compared trends in quality from those ship classes where multiple ships were delivered during this time period. To determine the number and type of deficiencies for each vessel, we obtained and analyzed data from the Navy's Board of Inspection and Survey's (INSURV) Material Inspection data warehouse and the Navy's Technical Support Management (TSM) system. TSM is the primary database SUPSHIP uses for tracking the status of new construction deficiencies. We reviewed these data for completeness, and when we identified obvious discrepancies we brought them to the attention of Navy officials and worked with them to understand, correct, or omit the discrepancies. We determined that the deficiency data we obtained were sufficiently reliable for the purposes of this report with two exceptions. These exceptions relate to data for T-AKE class ships. TSM data did not cover T-AKE 1 through T-AKE 6. In addition, data for T-AKE 12 had numerous data errors and is therefore not reported on. For other T-AKE ships, we reviewed deficiency documentation (trial cards) to resolve discrepancies between TSM and T-AKE program office data.

We visited eight U.S. private shipyards that build Navy ships and spoke with shipyard representatives. We also met with officials and analyzed data provided by several Navy organizations, including each of the SUPSHIP commands and detachments; INSURV; Program Executive Offices and shipbuilding programs; lifecycle and maintenance organizations; Fleet Forces Command; the Military Sealift Command; Navy Sea Systems Command Engineering, Contracting, and Logistics directorates, among others. We catalogued several hull, mechanical, and electrical quality problems with each ship class delivered since 2006. To create this list of illustrative examples, we asked Navy officials and shipbuilding contractor representatives to identify quality problems on these vessels. Further, this list focused only on quality issues that pertain to the construction of the hull, mechanical, and electrical systems; we did not include quality issues with weapons systems or other warfighting systems. We also reviewed the Navy's Back to Basics initiative and outcomes, as well as other recent efforts to improve the quality of shipbuilding.

To learn about practices used by leading commercial ship buyers and shipbuilders to ensure quality in new construction vessels, we spoke with leading buyers and shipbuilders in the cruise, oil and gas, and commercial shipping industries and reviewed our previous shipbuilding best practices work. Where possible, we collected documentation and/or witnessed quality assurance practices. For the purposes of this review, the leading commercial ship buyers we spoke with are companies that we identified as leaders in their industry in terms of being top operators of cruise ships, oil and gas vessels or containerships, and that agreed to participate in our review. We reviewed such indicators as annual sales, number of vessels owned or procured, and total market share. Leading commercial shipbuilders in this review were also identified as high quality shipbuilders by the ship buyers in our review or shipbuilding experts we met with. The firms participating in our review included Carnival Corporation, Chevron Corporation, Daewoo Shipbuilding and Marine Engineering, Ensco plc, ExxonMobil, Hyundai Heavy Industries, A.P. Moller-Maersk A/S, Meyer Werft, Noble Corporation, Norwegian Cruise Line, Royal Caribbean Cruises, Ltd., Seadrill Ltd., and STX Finland. We requested deficiency data from the commercial ship buyers for one or more new construction ships they acquired. With the exception of one floating production storage and offloading vessel, all of these ships were delivered to the buyers in 2012 or 2013. We assessed the reliability of these data by obtaining information on the systems that stored the data and interviewing ship buyer representatives knowledgeable about the data. We determined that the data were sufficiently reliable for the purposes of this report. We also identified common processes and tools used by these ship buyers and shipbuilders to ensure the expected level of quality. To determine the extent to which Navy quality assurance processes used commercial best practices, we reviewed data and information obtained from the Navy and its shipbuilding contractors as well as from the leading commercial ship buyers and shipbuilders. We also held meetings with SUPSHIP, program, and contracting officials about the Navy's quality practices and during our site visits to the U.S. shipyards. We discussed with shipyard representatives their quality assurance processes and the steps taken to ensure ships meet the Navy's quality expectations.

To better understand the role of classification societies in Navy and commercial shipbuilding, including the American Bureau of Shipping (ABS), we met with engineering and marine surveying representatives from ABS at the Navy contractor shipyards where they maintain a presence to obtain an overview of how they conduct their work. We also held discussions with officials from several Navy organizations, including SUPSHIP and Naval Sea Systems Command Engineering Directorate, as well as representatives from Navy shipbuilding contractors on the role of ship classification in Navy shipbuilding. We reviewed the classification rule set developed by the Navy and ABS for the Navy's surface combatants, as well as other classification rule sets pertaining to Navy and commercial vessels. We also spoke with representatives from other classification societies, including Det Norske Veritas and Lloyd's Register, to discuss their approach to classification of commercial and navy vessels, and met with commercial ship buyers and shipbuilders to discuss the classification process.

Appendix I contains additional detail on our scope and methodology.

We conducted this performance audit from March 2012 to November 2013 in accordance with generally accepted government auditing standards. Those standards require that we plan and perform the audit to obtain sufficient, appropriate evidence to provide a reasonable basis for our findings and conclusions based on our audit objectives. We believe that the evidence obtained provides a reasonable basis for our findings and conclusions based on our audit objectives.

Background

In general, a quality product is one that performs as expected and can be depended on to perform when needed. A quality product is also one that is free of deficiencies. For the purposes of this review, we define deficiencies as items that require corrective action to bring the material condition or performance of a product into compliance with required standards.[2]

---

[2]A variety of terms are often used to indicate a work item is deficient, such as defect, nonconformance, corrective work or corrective action, and items included on a "punch" list (essentially a list of all remaining work and corrective work necessary to meet the ship buyer's requirements). Remaining work or incomplete work refers to work that has yet to be performed in order to make a finished product or previously identified deficiencies that have yet to be corrected.

Performance, cost, schedule, and quality goals are interrelated. Improving quality within an organization to achieve the desired level of performance and reliability requires time and money in the short term. But in the longer term, such efforts can reduce costs and production times, as process-related costs—such as labor and materials needed to correct defects—are reduced or eliminated. Such production efficiencies have been demonstrated by companies that have successfully implemented quality philosophies, including the Six Sigma methodology.[3] Six Sigma and other quality philosophies establish a framework by which the process of production can be made more consistent by determining and eliminating the root causes of process-related problems, resulting in improved quality. Figure 1 demonstrates the interrelationship between schedule, cost, performance and quality.

Figure 1: Quality's Integral Role in Achieving Schedule, Cost, and Performance and Reliability Goals

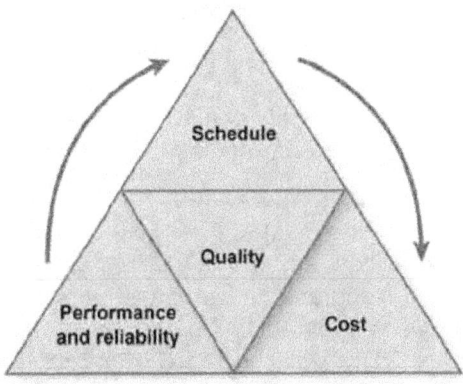

Source: GAO analysis of American Society of Quality data.

Shipbuilding is a major undertaking within the Navy, and several Navy organizations are involved, either directly or indirectly, with the acquisition, construction, and fielding of new ships. To some extent, all of the organizations described below have a role in helping to ensure the Navy acquires ships that meet quality expectations.

---

[3]The American Society for Quality defines Six Sigma as a fact based, data driven philosophy of quality improvement that values defect prevention over defect detection by reducing variation and waste in a process.

- **SUPSHIP** is the Navy's primary on-site representative at the private shipyards that build Navy ships, and is tasked with overseeing the shipbuilder's production processes. Services provided by SUPSHIP include contract administration, project management, engineering surveillance, quality assurance, logistics, and financial administration of assigned shipbuilding contracts. Typical work activities performed by SUPSHIP's quality assurance department include the following:

  - Quality assurance planning activities, such as oversight plans for monitoring the shipbuilder's quality program and periodic surveillance plans identifying the areas where quality assurance personnel will be allocated.
  - Reviews of the shipbuilding contractor's quality management system and work procedures.
  - Inspection and testing of the shipbuilder's completed work, including physical inspections, verifications, and equipment testing, as well as witnessing or monitoring the ship construction process.
  - Audits and inspections of the shipbuilder's work procedures to verify that personnel are complying with the procedures.
  - Evaluating the results of (1) SUPSHIP's quality inspections to identify quality trends and (2) quality and test data the shipbuilder is contractually required to provide the Navy.

- **Program Executive Offices (PEO),** and the program managers that report to them, are responsible for all aspects of life-cycle management of their assigned shipbuilding programs, including program initiation, ship design, construction, testing, delivery, fleet introduction, and maintenance activities.

- **The Navy's Board of Inspection and Survey (INSURV)** is an independent organization that inspects newly constructed and in-service Navy ships to determine their material condition and reports these assessments to Congress and Navy leadership.

- **The Naval Sea Systems Command Contracting Directorate (NAVSEA 02)** awards contracts worth about $24 billion annually for new construction ships and submarines, ship repair, major weapon systems, and services.

- **The Naval Sea Systems Command Engineering Directorate (NAVSEA 05)** provides the engineering and scientific expertise and technical authority for the Navy's ships, submarines, and associated warfare systems.

- **The Naval Sea Systems Command Nuclear Propulsion Directorate (NAVSEA 08)** is responsible for all aspects of the Navy's nuclear propulsion ships, including research, design, construction, and operations.

- **The Military Sealift Command** operates and maintains approximately 119 non-combatant Navy ships that deliver supplies to US forces and conduct specialized missions, such as supporting humanitarian aid efforts. Unlike other Navy ships, the ships are generally manned by civilian mariners. During construction of these vessels, the Command assigns a construction oversight representative at the shipyard to monitor compliance with requirements.
- **The Naval Sea Systems Command Surface Warfare Directorate (NAVSEA 21)** and **Undersea Warfare Directorate (NAVSEA 07)** provide life-cycle support for the Navy's surface combatants and submarines from when they are introduced into the fleet until they are no longer in service. In addition, the directorates provide the shipbuilding and submarine program offices with information on quality problems and lessons learned from ship deployments that may be used to improve the construction of subsequent vessels.
- **The Defense Contract Management Agency** administers contracts when delegated that authority by the contracting office. SUPSHIP commands generally delegate quality oversight of shipbuilding parts and equipment suppliers to the Defense Contract Management Agency.

Figure 2 depicts how those Navy organizations fit within the overall organizational structure of the Navy.

Figure 2: Simplified Organizational Chart of Navy Organizations Involved in the Construction of New Navy Ships

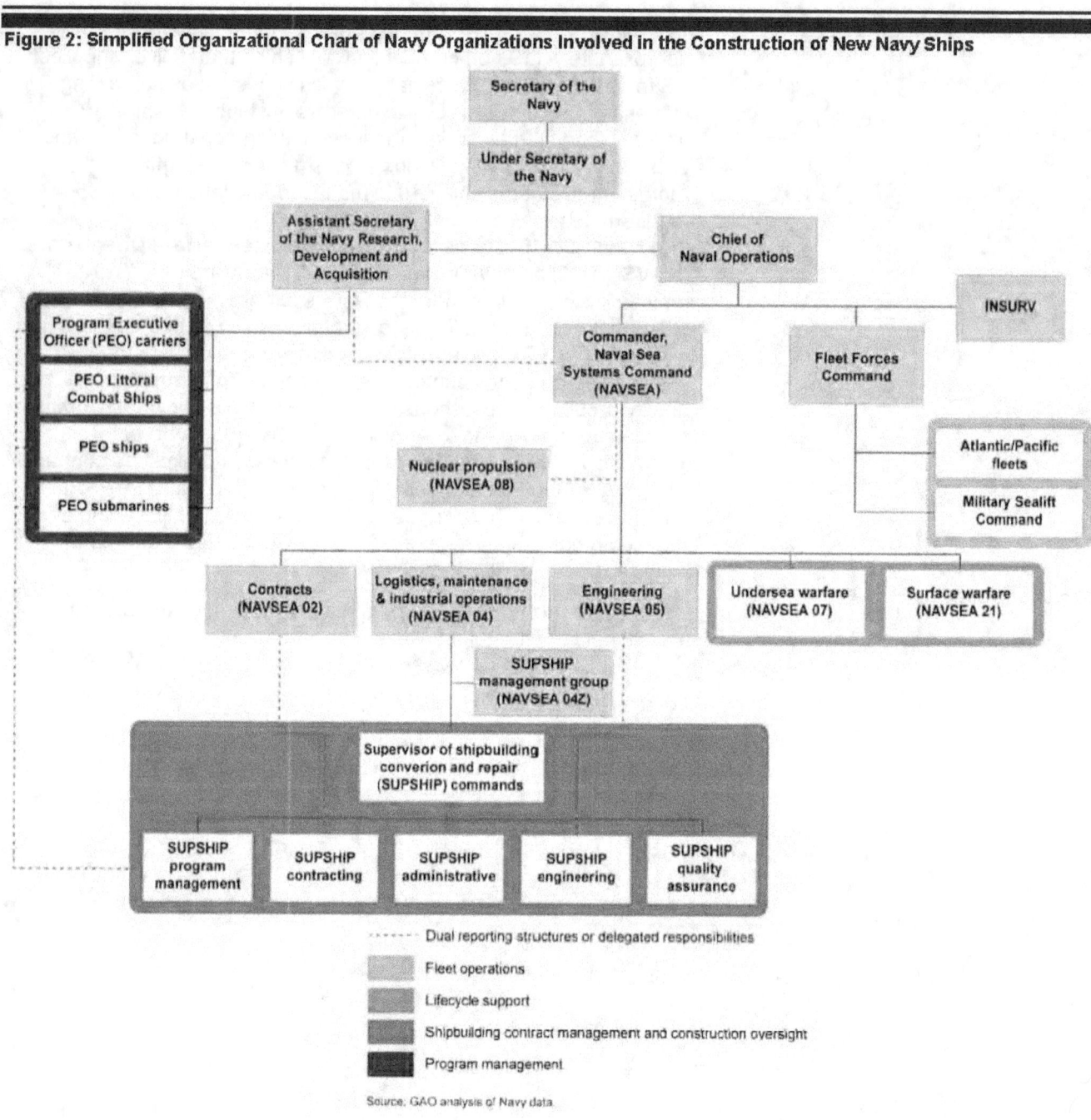

Source: GAO analysis of Navy data.

Stages of Shipbuilding

Shipbuilding is a complex, multistage industrial activity that includes a number of key events that are common regardless of the type of ship constructed or whether the buyer is the government or a commercial firm. These events are sequenced among four primary phases: pre-contracting, contract award, design and planning, and construction, with each successive phase building upon the work completed in earlier stages.[4]

In the pre-contracting stage, the ship buyer determines the ship's requirements. Early-stage design work occurs that culminates in a set of specifications that documents the buyer's requirements. In the contract award phase, the specifications are incorporated into the shipbuilding contract that the buyer enters into with the selected shipbuilder(s). After entering into the shipbuilding contract, the design and planning phase begins. The ship's detailed engineering design is completed—often in the form of a three-dimensional computer aided design model—and consists of developing all aspects of the ship's structures and the routing of major distributive systems, such as electrical work or piping. Any necessary modeling and simulation analyses, such as testing the structural integrity of the design over the service life of the ship, are also completed. In addition, during this stage the shipbuilder plans for beginning construction and generates two-dimensional drawings that, once approved by the ship buyer, will be used by production workers to build the ship.

Ship construction involves the following key events:

- **Block fabrication, assembly, outfitting, and erection:** Metal plates are welded together into elements called blocks—the basic building units for a ship. Blocks are generally outfitted with pipes, brackets for machinery or cabling, ladders, and any other equipment that may be available for installation at this early stage of construction. The blocks are then welded together to form grand blocks and erected with other grand blocks in a drydock or building area. Outfitting work, painting, and pre-commissioning activities take place prior to sea trials.
- **Sea trials:** Once the shipbuilder is satisfied that the ship is completed, the ship embarks on a series of dockside and at-sea tests to evaluate overall quality and performance against the contractually required technical specifications and buyer's performance requirements. Navy shipbuilding programs generally conduct two sets of sea trials—

---

[4]See appendix II, table 2 for a more detailed description of these phases.

builder's trials and acceptance trials.[5] SUPSHIP inspectors are generally responsible for observing and identifying deficiencies during the builder's sea trials, while acceptance trials are observed by inspectors from INSURV, the Navy's inspection board.

- **Delivery / acceptance:** Following the successful completion of sea trials and when the buyer is satisfied that the ship meets requirements, the shipyard delivers the ship to the buyer. In Navy shipbuilding, the official transfer of custody occurs when the Navy signs a Material Inspection and Receiving Report (Form DD 250).

Post-delivery activities that are specific to Navy shipbuilding, which can generally take up to a year to complete, include the following:

- **Final outfitting, post-delivery tests:** Following delivery and until the ship sails away from the shipbuilder's yard—usually anywhere from 10 to 90 days after delivery—the crew boards the ship and begins training, and the ship's mission systems are installed. Additional training and operational tests of mission systems occur at the ship's home port.[6]
- **Final contract trials:** INSURV inspectors conduct a second round of sea trials to assess whether the ship and all mission equipment are operating as intended.
- **Post Shakedown Availability:** A period of planned maintenance follows final contract trials. During this time, class-wide upgrades and correction of new or previously identified deficiencies that are the government's responsibility also occur.
- **Obligation and Work Limiting Date:** The official date on which full responsibility for funding the ship's operation and maintenance is transferred from the acquisition command to the operational fleet.

Construction-related quality deficiencies on Navy ships can be identified at all points throughout the shipbuilding process, from initial block fabrication to sea trials up through delivery. During acceptance trials, INSURV inspectors label the most serious issues as "starred" deficiencies. These issues can significantly degrade a ship's ability to perform an assigned primary or secondary operational capability or the

---

[5]In some instances, commercial ships, such as liquefied natural gas carriers or drill ships, may undergo additional sea trials following delivery to test specific equipment related to the ships' missions and intended uses.

[6]On nuclear powered Navy ships, the ship's crew begins boarding and training prior to ship delivery.

crew's ability to safely operate and maintain ship systems. Because of their importance, starred deficiencies must be corrected by the builder or waived by the Chief of Naval Operations prior to ship delivery.

In addition to starred deficiencies, INSURV inspectors categorize other types of deficiencies—each of which represent a piece of the vessel that is not in compliance with Navy standards and/or contract specifications at the time of inspection. While not deemed as serious as starred deficiencies, these items can nonetheless affect the quality of life and safety of the sailors on board the vessel or the operability of the ship. INSURV categorizes these issues into three parts based on the professional judgment of its inspectors:

- **Part I deficiencies** are very significant in that they are likely to cause the ship to be unseaworthy or to substantially reduce the ship's ability to carry out its assigned mission. "Part I Safety" is a sub-category that INSURV uses to indicate that an issue is severe enough that the ship is unsafe to operate until corrected. All starred deficiencies are Part I deficiencies but not all Part I deficiencies are starred. An example of a Part I starred deficiency would be an anchor that when deployed during testing was not fully retrievable.
- **Part II deficiencies** involve less significant material degradation but should be corrected to restore the ship to required specifications. Part II deficiencies can also have a safety designation. Examples are wide ranging and can include items such as missing signage, or areas of the ship having missing or damaged paint and coatings.
- **Part III deficiencies** are generally categorized as things that prevent the ship from meeting Navy standards but are cost prohibitive to fix. An example is a lifeboat compartment that is too small to fit the size of a lifeboat necessary to meet Navy requirements.

While INSURV inspectors identify deficiencies during acceptance trials, throughout the ship construction process SUPSHIP quality inspectors, during the normal course of their work, may observe work being performed that is not in accordance with the technical specifications, quality requirements included in the contract between the Navy and the shipbuilder, or the shipbuilder's work procedures. In such instances, SUPSHIP inspectors will issue a request for the builder to correct the deficient work. Depending on the severity and extent of the problems, SUPSHIP's quality officials may send a request for corrective action to the builder to determine the cause of the problems, correct the affected work, and improve its work processes so that the problems will not reoccur. Once the shipbuilder takes the appropriate actions, SUPSHIP closes out the corrective action request. At the time of the builder's sea trials, any unresolved SUPSHIP requests for corrective action are generally grouped together with deficiencies identified by SUPSHIP inspectors during the builder's sea trials process.[7]

Navy Shipbuilding Environment

As opposed to the commercial buyers included in our review, which typically operate in a robust, competitive environment, the Navy has a limited industrial base to build its ships. For example, throughout the world there are at least 12 shipbuilding and offshore marine companies that ship buyers in the oil and gas sector can choose from to build their vessels. In contrast, two U.S. Navy shipbuilding contractors—General Dynamics and Huntington Ingalls Industries—own all but three of the larger shipyards, and each yard is specialized to build specific types of ships. For example, aircraft carriers can only be built at one location. In addition to building Navy ships, two of the shipyards, General Dynamics NASSCO and V.T. Halter Marine, also build vessels for commercial shipping firms. Figure 3 depicts the major U.S. shipbuilders and the types of ships they build.

[7]On non-nuclear ships, when deficiencies identified during the builder's sea trials are not resolved prior to acceptance trials, some of the uncorrected deficiencies are transferred and grouped together with the deficiencies INSURV inspectors identify during the acceptance trials process, if the inspectors determine that the deficiencies pertain to Navy operational capabilities, contracted requirements, and safety regulations.

Figure 3: Locations of Major Navy Contractor Shipyards and Associated Product Lines

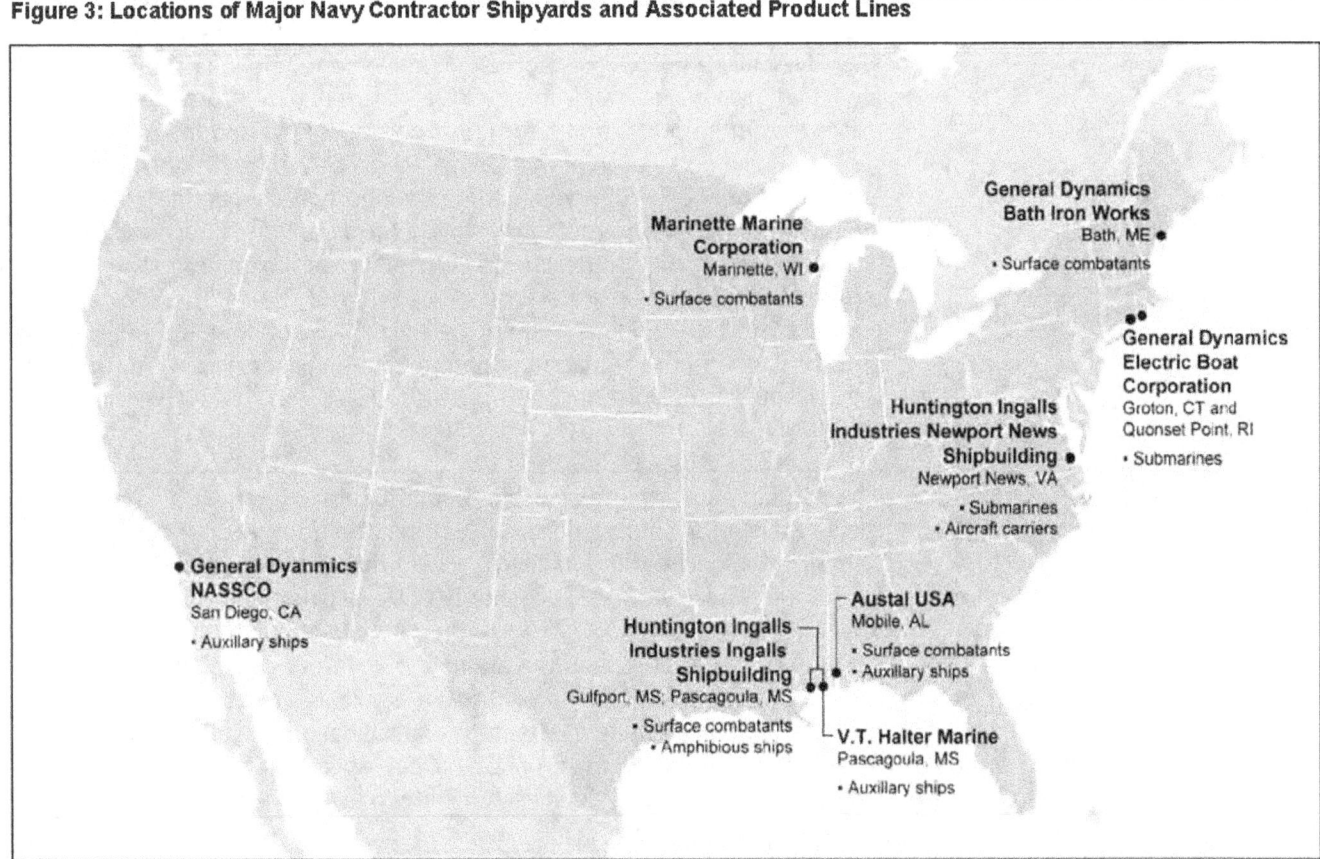

Note: Auxiliary ships include transport, cargo, and ammunition ships.

The Navy uses several different types of contracts for shipbuilding programs. The Navy will often use cost-reimbursement contracts for the first ships of a new class, as in many instances the Navy and its shipbuilding contractors do not have a full understanding of the costs and effort needed to build and deliver the ships. Such contracts provide for payment of allowable incurred costs, to the extent prescribed in the contract. The Navy also typically includes incentive or award fees on these contracts. Our prior work has shown that this type of contract places more cost risk on the government in the event that the shipbuilder is unable to deliver the ship on time and within budget.[8] For shipbuilding programs where the Navy has greater certainty about costs and risks, the Navy typically employs fixed-price-incentive contracts. Fixed-price-incentive (firm target) contracts include a target cost, target profit, ceiling price (maximum price) and a formula used to determined the shipbuilder's profit that are negotiated at the outset. Final costs that are above the target cost but below the ceiling price are shared between the Navy and shipbuilder through the profit adjustment formula. If the final costs exceed the ceiling price, the shipbuilder is generally responsible for most additional costs. In some instances the Navy will use a firm-fixed-price contract, in which the final price of the ship is agreed to at the outset. This contract type generally places upon the contractor maximum risk and full responsibility for all costs.

Classification Societies

The maritime industry has certain requirements to ensure ships meet a minimum level of safety and quality. Under the International Maritime Organization conventions, uniform requirements have been established to, among other things, ensure safety of life while at sea and environmental protection.[9] These requirements stipulate that ships are designed, constructed, and maintained in accordance with the rules of a recognized classification society or with applicable national standards that provide an equivalent level of safety. Classification societies, such as the American Bureau of Shipping (ABS), Det Norske Veritas, and Lloyd's Register, develop rules defining a minimum level of technical standards that are applied to ships. Once a ship is "classed" with a certificate indicating that it meets a minimum level of safety and quality, the ship is subject to periodic inspection to verify that it continues to meet the applicable rules of the issuing classification society. In many instances, shipbuilders also use classification societies to audit their quality management systems as an independent third-party, which often is needed to maintain certain certifications such as the International

---

[8]See GAO-09-322 and, GAO, *Defense Acquisitions: Improved Management Practices Could Help Minimize Cost Growth in Navy Shipbuilding Programs*, GAO-05-183 (Washington, D.C.: Feb. 28, 2005).

[9]The International Maritime Organization is the United Nations' organization responsible for maritime affairs and develops international treaties in this area. For example, the Safety of Life at Sea Convention is generally regarded as the most important of all international treaties concerning the safety of commercial ships, and specifies minimum safety standards for the construction, equipment and operation of certain ships.

Organization for Standardization's ISO 9001 (quality), 14001 (environmental), and 18001 (occupational health and safety) series of management systems standards.[10]

Many of these international shipping requirements regarding classification do not apply to Navy ships.[11] However, in some instances the Navy voluntarily complies with certain maritime and commercial classification requirements, such as for ships operated by the Military Sealift Command.[12] Beginning in 2003, the Navy entered into an agreement with ABS to assist with redefining the Navy's standards for the design and construction of its non-nuclear surface combatant ships—surface ships that are designed to engage in attacks against land, air, and sea targets—to be more consistent with the classification process used on commercial and Military Sealift Command-operated ships. The result of this effort was development of the Naval Vessel Rules, which establish a minimum set of requirements for the basic construction of the Navy's surface combatant ships.[13] In addition, the Navy required shipbuilding contractors to contract with ABS to pilot the application and implementation of the Naval Vessel Rules on the USS *Zumwalt* (DDG 1000) and Littoral Combat Ship (LCS) shipbuilding programs. Under this arrangement, ABS involvement in the LCS and DDG 1000 programs is similar to that of a commercial shipbuilding project in which, throughout design and construction of the ship, the classification society acts as an independent third-party assessor to ensure the ship is in compliance with

---

[10]In particular, ISO 9001 certification is commonly obtained by all types of manufacturing and production companies and can indicate to potential customers that a company has established and implements a defined minimum level of quality policies and standards.

[11]Navy officials stated that the certification requirement for submarines is as rigorous as that of classification societies. During the design, construction, and maintenance of submarines, they use an oversight and certification program analogous to ship classification—called Submarine Safety—as a means to help ensure requirements are met and a minimum level of safety is achieved. The officials noted the Submarine Safety program is a cornerstone of the Navy's submarine design, construction, and maintenance practices and provides the basis for certification of every submarine.

[12]The Military Sealift Command is largely comprised of civilian staff and mariners. Since 1960, Military Sealift Command-operated ships have obtained and maintained commercial ship classification certificates issued by ABS. Section 3316 of title 46 of the U.S. code (as amended), designates ABS as the agency for ship classification and related functions for U.S. Government-owned vessels.

[13]American Bureau of Shipping, *The ABS Guide for Building and Classing Naval Vessels* (2004).

the applicable classification rule sets. Upon completion of all requirements, ABS issues a classification certificate.

The Navy Has Reduced Deficiencies at Delivery but Still Accepts Some Ships with Numerous Construction Deficiencies

Recognizing that it has experienced significant quality problems with several ship classes, the Navy has focused on reducing the number of serious deficiencies, particularly "starred" deficiencies, which require a waiver from the Chief of Naval Operations to defer correction until after delivery. The number of uncorrected deficiencies at delivery, including starred deficiencies, has generally dropped for ships delivered over the past few years due, at least in part, to the Back to Basics quality improvement initiative. Even so, the Navy still accepts some ships with large numbers of open deficiencies. Navy policy states that ships are to be delivered based on acceptance trials and satisfactory correction or resolution of deficiencies. Instead, correction of deficiencies is often deferred until after the Navy accepts delivery of the ship, which can interfere with post-delivery activities. Further, one product of the Back to Basics initiative, a quality management provision for inclusion in Navy shipbuilding contracts, has not been implemented on any Navy shipbuilding contract.

The Navy Has Reduced the Number of Starred Deficiencies at Delivery

The Navy has reduced the total number of uncorrected starred deficiencies at delivery on both established and newer ship classes for which multiple ships have been delivered. It is up to INSURV inspectors to categorize deficiencies identified by severity during acceptance trials. Because there can be ambiguity regarding who is responsible for correcting the deficiencies, the program office, SUPSHIP, and the shipbuilder collectively determine whether the government or the shipbuilding contractor is responsible. Deficiencies that the government is responsible for correcting can include, among other things, problems requiring a change to the ship design or ship specification, or equipment that the government is responsible for providing. For example, during the acceptance trial of LCS 2, the rescue boat could not be properly deployed and INSURV inspectors categorized the problem as a starred deficiency. It was subsequently determined that, as designed, the rescue boat system did not have the ability to meet requirements and that the Navy would assume responsibility for the corrective work. Figures 4 through 7 show the open number of starred deficiencies at delivery for the LPD 17, DDG 51, T-AKE, and LCS ship classes during the 2006 through 2012 time frame.[14] These are the classes of ships that had multiple vessels delivered in this time frame. The figures also show when the Back to Basics initiative began.

Figure 4: Open Starred Deficiencies at Delivery for LPD 17 Ship Class

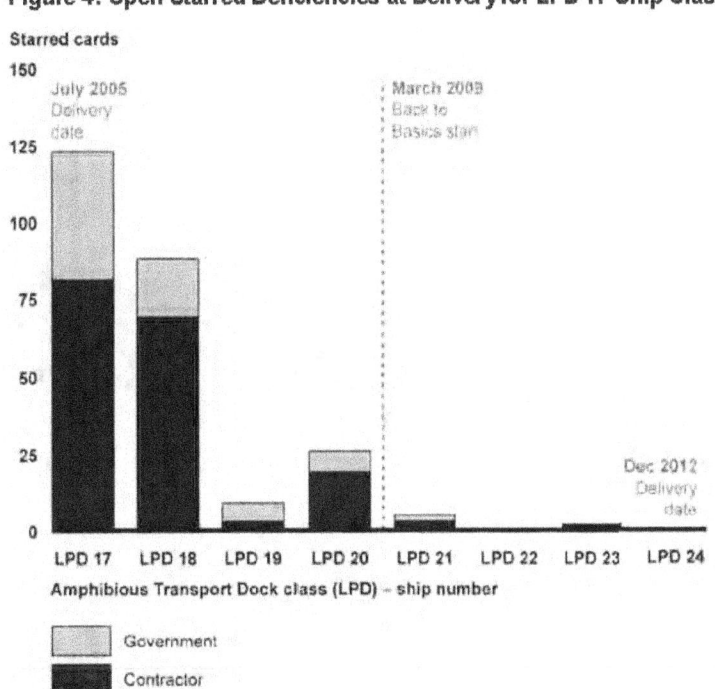

Starred cards

Amphibious Transport Dock class (LPD) – ship number

Government
Contractor

Source: GAO analysis of Navy data

Note: LPD 17 was delivered to the Navy in 2005, but is included in our analysis as this was the lead ship for the San Antonio class.

[14]Since 2006, the Virginia class submarine program has also delivered multiple vessels. According to the Navy, the Virginia class program is considered to be one of the Navy's most well run programs, but we did not compare it to the surface ships due to differences in the delivery process.

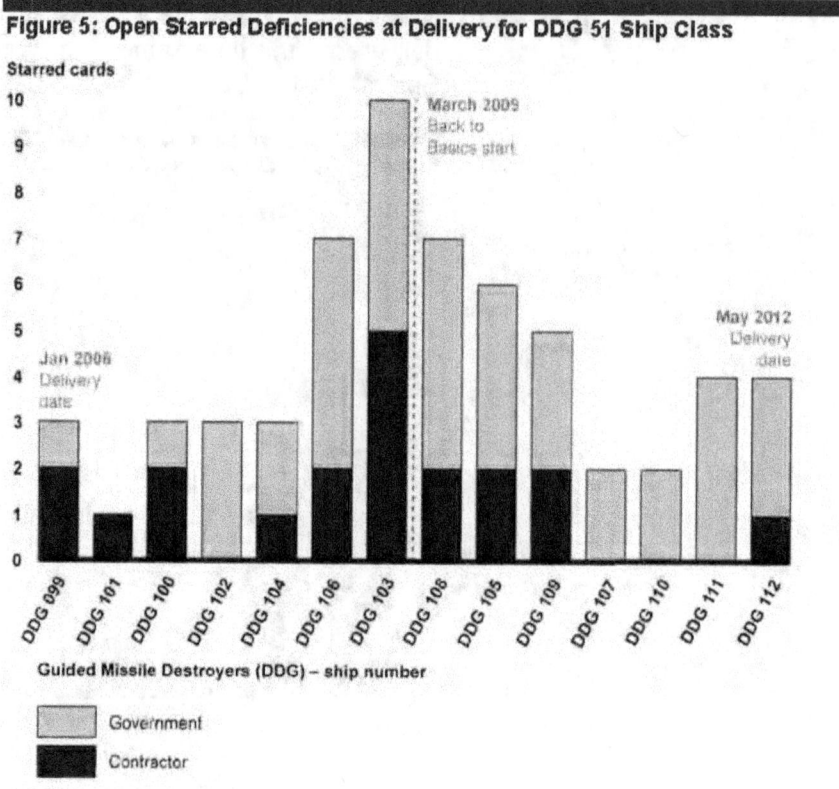

Figure 5: Open Starred Deficiencies at Delivery for DDG 51 Ship Class

Source: GAO analysis of Navy data.

Note: DDG 51 class ships are built at two Navy contractor shipyards in Bath, Maine and Pascagoula, Mississippi. Ships are presented in chronological order based on the date of delivery to the Navy.

Figure 6: Open Starred Deficiencies at Delivery for T-AKE Ship Class

Starred cards

5

4 March 2009
   Delivery date
   & Back to
   Basics start

3

2

1

Oct 2012
Delivery
date

0

 T-AKE 07 T-AKE 08 T-AKE 09 T-AKE 10 T-AKE 11 T-AKE 13 T-AKE 14

Dry cargo and ammunition ships (T-AKE) – ship number

☐ Government

■ Contractor

Source: GAO analysis of Navy data

Note: The database used for this analysis did not contain information on T-AKE 1 through T-AKE 6, delivered between 2006 and 2008. Data obtained for T-AKE 12 indicated that almost all of the deficiencies were opened and closed on the same day following the ship's delivery and, as such, data for that ship were deemed not sufficiently reliable for the purpose of this analysis.

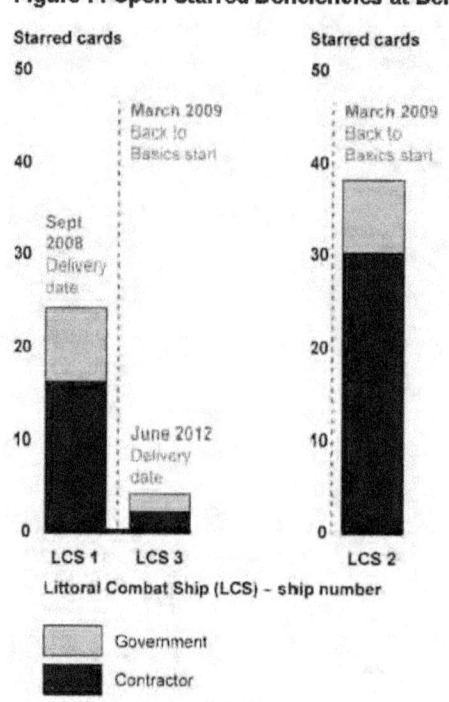

Figure 7: Open Starred Deficiencies at Delivery for LCS Ship Class

Source: GAO analysis of Navy data

Note: Odd numbered LCS class ships (*Freedom* variant) are built at a shipyard in Marinette, Wisconsin, while even numbered ships (*Independence* variant) are built at a shipyard in Mobile, Alabama.

In addition to starred deficiencies, total deficiencies have declined for several ship classes. Notably, the last ship of the T-AKE class, T-AKE 14, was delivered in 2012 with no deficiencies that the shipbuilder was responsible for correcting. Uncorrected deficiencies were also kept to a minimum on the recently delivered Joint High Speed Vessel and Mobile Landing Platform—both based on commercial designs and operated by the Military Sealift Command. The first Joint High Speed Vessel, an intratheater troop and cargo transport ship, was delivered in December 2012 with only 54 uncorrected deficiencies, of which 6 were categorized as Part I deficiencies. The first Mobile Landing Platform, which will provide at-sea cargo and equipment transfers, was delivered in May 2013 with only three uncorrected shipbuilder-responsible deficiencies, according to the Navy. These had not been resolved prior to delivery because the shipbuilder was waiting for parts to correct the items.

Figure 8 shows the number of open deficiencies at the time of delivery for the T-AKE ship class. The figure also shows when the Back to Basics initiative began. In addition, appendix III provides additional information on the numbers and types of deficiencies at different points in time for T-AKE class ships delivered to the Navy from 2009 through 2012.

Figure 8: Non-Starred Deficiencies at Time of Delivery for T-AKE Ship Class

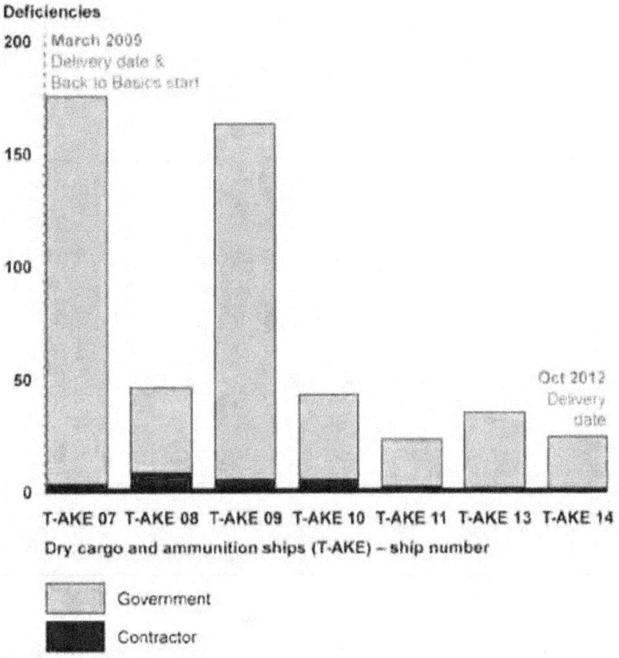

Source: GAO analysis of Navy data

Notes:

The database used for this analysis did not contain information on T-AKE 1 through T-AKE 6, delivered between 2006 and 2008. Data obtained for T-AKE 12 indicated that almost all of the deficiencies were opened and closed on the same day following the ship's delivery and as such, data for that ship were deemed not sufficiently reliable for the purpose of this analysis. In some instances, similar types of deficiencies were consolidated into a single deficiency prior to ship delivery. The data above contains deficiencies where it was subsequently determined no further corrective action would be taken.

It should be noted that a confluence of several factors led to improved quality for the T-AKE and Mobile Landing Platform ship classes. The quality of ships generally improves as ship classes mature. Production efficiencies are gained from process improvements and incorporation of lessons learned into the build strategy. During early production of the T-AKE ship class, the shipbuilder initiated shipyard-wide production improvements and other efficiencies resulting, in part, from the shipbuilder's partnership with a leading international commercial shipbuilder. With the improvement in quality, the T-AKE program moved to a contract type which transfers more of the cost risk resulting from any quality problems to the shipbuilder. Specifically, for T-AKE 10 through T-AKE 14 the Navy transitioned from a fixed-priced-incentive contract to a firm-fixed-price contract. The shipbuilder for the Mobile Landing Platform attributed the delivery of a nearly defect-free ship to its focus on ensuring that all design engineering efforts and production planning activities were fully completed prior to the start of the lead ship's construction. Shipbuilder representatives stated that this was a key factor in keeping rework rates for quality problems low.

Numbers of Other Deficiencies at Delivery Remains Substantial

Even with the drop in the number of starred deficiencies, the Navy has continued to accept delivery of some ships with large numbers of uncorrected deficiencies. For example, LPD 22, which was delivered without any starred deficiencies and was cited by Navy officials as a turning point for the LPD 17 ship class, had over 3,300 deficiencies that the contractor was responsible for correcting at delivery. Subsequent LPD ships, LPD 23 and 24, both delivered in 2012, had fewer but still sizeable numbers of uncorrected deficiencies. On these ships, examples of uncorrected Part II deficiencies that were the shipbuilder's responsibility when delivered included pipe hangers that were insufficiently spaced to support the weight intended or that did not meet the Navy's requirements; fire suppression sprinklers not providing adequate coverage due to obstructions and interference from pipes and ductwork; and inability to fully extend a crane boom due to overhead obstructions on LPD 24. While Part II deficiencies are considered to be not as severe as Part I deficiencies, these deficiencies nonetheless can require a fair amount of shipbuilder effort to remedy.

Figure 9 shows the total number of open non-starred deficiencies (Part I, Part II, and Part III) at the time of delivery for the LPD 17 ship class. The figure also shows when the Back to Basics initiative began. Appendix IV provides additional information on the numbers and types of deficiencies at different points in time for LPD class ships delivered to the Navy since 2009, when the Back to Basics initiative began.

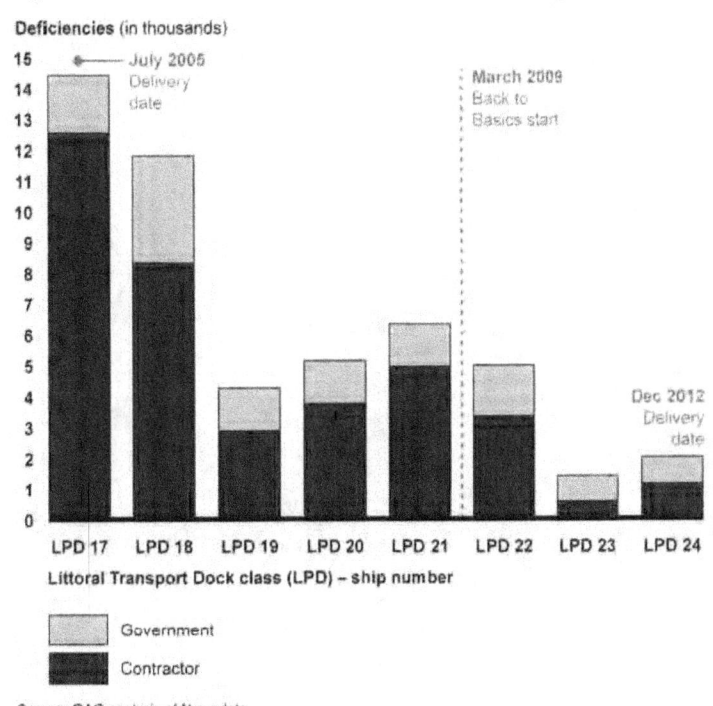

Figure 9: Non-Starred Deficiencies at Time of Delivery for LPD 17 Ship Class

Deficiencies (in thousands)

Littoral Transport Dock class (LPD) – ship number

- Government
- Contractor

Source: GAO analysis of Navy data

Notes:

LPD 17 was delivered to the Navy in 2005, but is included in our analysis as this was the lead ship for the San Antonio class.

Deficiencies closed up to 7 days after date of delivery are treated as being closed at delivery to account for potential lags in data entry.

As another example, on LCS 3, uncorrected Part II deficiencies that were the shipbuilder's responsibility at the time of delivery included use of incorrect weld-filler material on pipe joints associated with the ship's water jets; instances where cabling was insufficiently supported, was bent, or had insufficient banding; and valves that were inaccessible due to obstructions.

Figure 10 summarizes the number of open non-starred deficiencies (Part I, Part II, and Part III) at the time of delivery for the LCS ship class. The figure also shows when the Back to Basics initiative began. In addition, appendix V provides additional information on the numbers and types of deficiencies at different points in time for the LCS ship class.

Figure 10: Non-Starred Deficiencies at Time of Delivery for LCS Ship Class

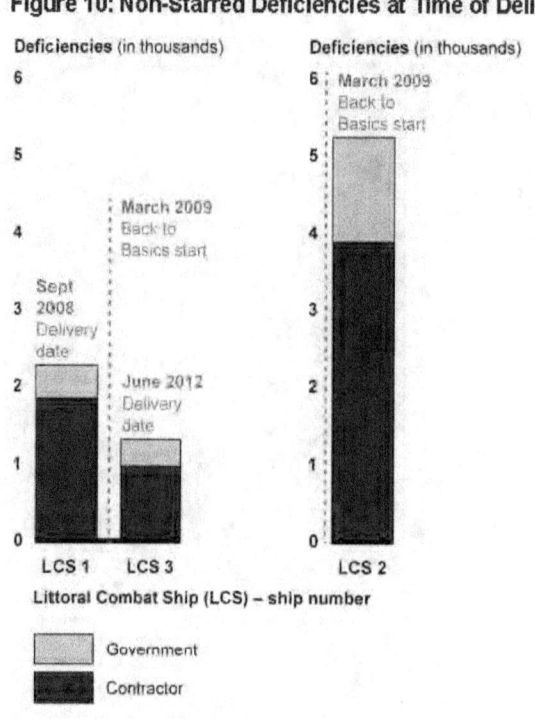

Source: GAO analysis of Navy data.

Notes:

Odd numbered LCS ships (*Freedom* variant) are built at a Navy contractor shipyard in Marinette, Wisconsin, while even numbered ships (*Independence* variant) are built at a Navy contractor shipyard in Mobile, Alabama.

Deficiencies closed up to 7 days after date of delivery are treated as being closed at delivery to account for potential lags in data entry.

In the above examples for the LPD and LCS ship classes, many of the deficiencies were first identified by SUPSHIP inspectors either prior to or during the builders' sea trials but were not corrected before delivery.

In addition, correcting very significant deficiencies (Part I) can require various levels of effort. For example, INSURV designated a broken window in the helicopter control station as a Part I deficiency on DDG 112. This may be relatively easy to fix, but is labeled a Part I deficiency because, according to deficiency documentation, until this issue is corrected the aviation facilities on the vessel cannot be fully certified, limiting operations. However, other issues could be more complex to correct. On DDG 108, for example, INSURV inspectors identified locations within the ship where there was insufficient corrosion protection, which if left uncorrected could result in accelerated corrosion as it did on at least one previous hull. Additional corrosion protection features were necessary to correct the issue, resulting in changes to the ship specification for follow-on hulls. Figure 11 summarizes the number of open non-starred deficiencies (Part I, Part II, and Part III) at the time of delivery for the DDG 51 ship class. The figure also shows when the Back to Basics initiative began. Appendix VI provides additional information on the numbers and types of deficiencies at different points in time for those DDG 51 class ships delivered to the Navy since 2009, when the Back to Basics initiative began.

Figure 11: Non-Starred Deficiencies at Time of Delivery for DDG 51 Ship Class

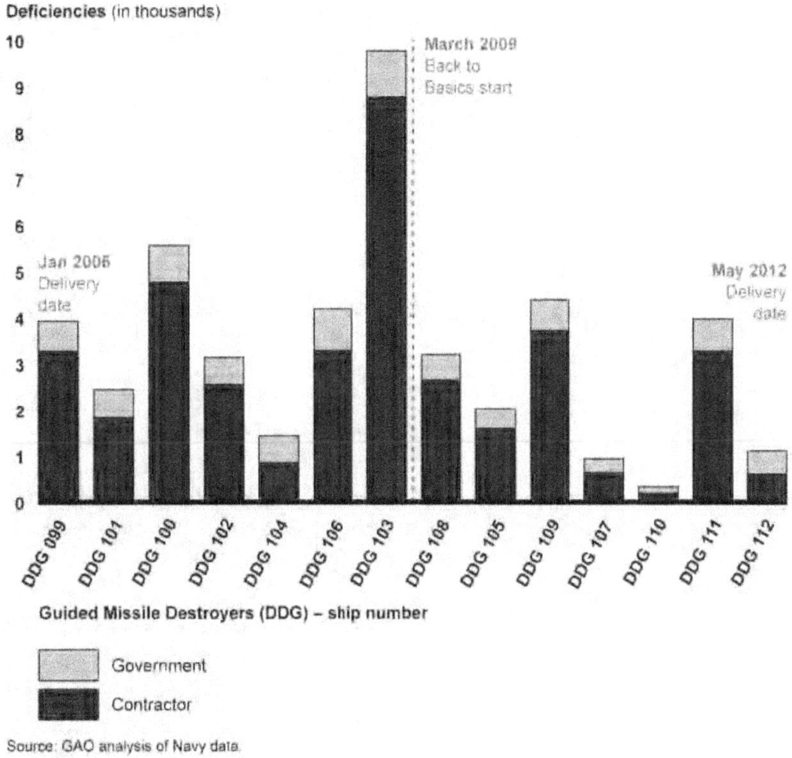

Deficiencies (in thousands)

Guided Missile Destroyers (DDG) – ship number

Government
Contractor

Source: GAO analysis of Navy data.

Notes:

DDG 51 class ships are built at two Navy contractor shipyards in Bath, Maine and Pascagoula, Mississippi. Ships are presented in chronological order based on the date delivered to the Navy.

Deficiencies closed up to 7 days after date of delivery are treated as being closed at delivery to account for potential lags in data entry.

While our analysis indicates that deficiencies have generally been decreasing where there are multiple ships in a class, we found instances where ships built individually or infrequently experienced difficulties in meeting the Navy's requirements prior to being delivered to the Navy. These include the *Wasp* class amphibious assault ship (LHD 8), the *Nimitz* class aircraft carrier (CVN 77), and a missile instrumentation ship (T-AGM 25).

- The Navy accepted delivery of LHD 8 in April 2009 with over 12,000 uncorrected deficiencies which were determined to be the shipbuilder's responsibility. Of these, almost 70 percent were for items SUPSHIP inspectors had identified before or during the builder's sea trials, including numerous deficiencies related to the ship's cabling and wiring. According to representatives of the shipbuilder, following delivery the shipbuilder undertook an intensive effort lasting several months to assess the condition of the ship's cabling, as it was unclear which cables and wires were properly routed. As a result of the costs incurred by the shipbuilder for this effort, the builder completely revised and modernized the approach used to install cables and wires on subsequent ships built at the shipyard.

- According to the shipbuilder's list of incomplete work items and deficiencies, the Navy took delivery of CVN 77 in May 2009, with about 7 percent of the ship's compartments unfinished; over 8,000 uncorrected deficiencies that had been identified prior to or during sea trials; and approximately 3,900 generally minor deficiencies (such as missing cable tags and electrical outlets) that were identified by the crew during its inspection. In addition, INSURV inspectors noted during CNV 77's acceptance trial that because the ship was not fully primed and painted, longer-term cost and maintenance implications needed to be addressed, as corrosion developed in the unfinished spaces and machinery.

- During the May 2011 acceptance trial for T-AGM 25, INSURV inspectors recommended that the Navy not take delivery of the ship until an additional acceptance trial was conducted because almost none of the major systems on the vessel were in satisfactory condition, and several were incomplete or inoperable. The inspectors also noted that most of the deficiencies they cited were previously identified during builder's trials but had not been properly corrected and retested. In the months following, the shipbuilder conducted an additional builder's trial to demonstrate some key components along with INSURV's second acceptance trial. At the time of delivery in January 2012, there were 67 unresolved deficiencies from sea trials which the shipbuilding contractor was responsible for correcting, and about 600 additional items identified by the Navy requiring correction by the builder, including improperly secured and supported cables, damaged paint, missing safety equipment, and loose tiles.

In these cases, the Navy gave priority to programmatic goals and determined it was in the best interest of the Navy to proceed with key milestones despite a large volume of uncorrected deficiencies or incomplete work. According to Navy officials, the Navy may make such determinations based on its strategic needs or additional costs that may be incurred by not proceeding with key milestones. For example, the LHD 8 program office took delivery of the ship as it was over a year and half behind schedule, primarily due to lingering effects from Hurricane Katrina, a shipyard-wide strike, and delays completing the ship's machinery control system. With CVN 77, SUPSHIP and program office officials stated it was necessary to take delivery of the ship in its unfinished condition so that it could periodically participate in training missions while the remaining work was being completed. Lastly, program officials decided to proceed with acceptance trials for T-AGM 25 to meet scheduling constraints associated with installation of the ship's mission package at another location, which could only be accomplished after taking delivery of the ship. In addition, SUPSHIP officials noted that in some instances, such as with T-AGM 25, the decision was made to proceed with sea trials in an effort to reveal additional problems with the ship that may not have been known at the time.

Deficiencies May Persist into Operations

Deficiencies identified by SUPSHIP and INSURV, if not sufficiently corrected, may link to problems later when the ship is in operation. In some instances, issues identified by SUPSHIP's quality inspectors during construction were closed prior to delivery—indicating the builder had satisfactorily addressed the problems—but the root causes of the problems were not fully resolved. For example, during the construction of DDG 107 issues with welding were identified in the normal course of SUPSHP's quality inspections. Specifically, SUPSHIP inspectors identified weld defects on the ship's mast and issued a request for corrective action to the shipbuilder. The action was closed, indicating that the builder had resolved the identified problems. However, during a routine training exercise in February 2011, a sub-section of the ship's mast failed when the welds could no longer support the structure. According to Navy investigators, it is likely that the section of the mast would have fallen onto the ship or into the water, but cables prevented it from falling. Although the section of the mast that failed was not at the same location where defective welds were identified by SUPSHIP, a Navy investigation into the issue identified several causes of the failure, including inadequate quality assurance oversight by the shipbuilder and poor workmanship during the construction process.

In addition, deficiencies can also combine to form larger issues. Quality problems that stem from deficiencies are often complex and can manifest long after the error occurred that led to the problem. Navy documents addressing quality concerns state that hull, mechanical, and electrical issues are often the result of one or more of the following causes:

- Construction and workmanship deficiencies, such as weld defects or inadequate painting;
- Design errors, such as refueling at sea systems that cannot accommodate necessary fuel offloading rates; and
- Supplier and subcontractor issues, such as counterfeit parts and sub-systems that do not work properly.

For example, a gas turbine engine on LCS 1 was ruined and had to be replaced because it was flooded with sea water. The Navy determined that this occurred because (1) the welds for the doors and water separators were not flush, creating gaps that allowed water to pass through the doors (a workmanship issue); (2) there were gaps in the sealing surfaces of the water separator that also allowed water to penetrate (a design issue); and (3) a key filter became clogged because it was not replaced in a timely manner (a maintenance issue).

Figure 12 catalogues select quality problems for a number of ships related to hull, mechanical, and electrical workmanship that persisted following delivery of the vessels. To generate this list, we asked Navy officials from many different departments, including program offices, maintenance units, and ship operators, to identify problems facing the various ship classes built in the last eight years.

Figure 12: Shipbuilding Issues

Interactive Graphic   lick on an image to see more detailed information about each ship. For print version, please see Appendix VII.

CVN 77
USS George H.W. Bush, Nimitz
lass Aircraft arrier

DDG 51
USS Arleigh Burke Guided Missile
Destroyer hip lass

LCS 1
USS Freedom
ittoral ombat hip lass

uality problems have affected the basic construction of all classes of Navy ships delivered in the last 8 years—from 2004 to 2012. Basic construction includes all aspects of constructing the ship's main structure (hull), mechanical and electrical systems, and primarily consists of welding blocks of steel and pipes, outfitting the ship with major systems (such as the propulsion system), and wiring the ship with various types of cables. This following graphic illustrates some of these quality issues.

LCS 2
USS Independence
ittoral ombat hip lass

LHD 8
USS Makin Island, Wasp   lass
Amphibious Assault hip

LPD 17 – 24
Amphibious Transport Dock lass

SSN 774
USS Virginia –
lass Fast Attack ubmarines

T-AGM 25
USNS Howard O. Lorenzen
Missile Instrumentation hip

T-AKE
USNS Lewis and Clark Dry argo
and Ammunition hip lass

ource GAO analysis of Navy data (data and images).

Accepting a Vessel with Deficiencies Is Common, and Varying Interpretations of Policy Dictate Practice

Policy issued by the Office of the Chief of Naval Operations (*Navy Instruction 4700.8J, Trials, Acceptance, Commissioning, Fitting Out, Shakedown, and Post Shakedown Availability of U.S. Naval Ships Undergoing Construction or Conversion*) states the following:

- For new construction ships, all contractual and governmental responsibilities should be resolved prior to delivery, except for crew certification, outfitting, or special Navy range requirements which cannot be met until after delivery.
- Delivery of the ship is based on acceptance trials and satisfactory correction or resolution of deficiencies, and acceptance trials shall be conducted when all work, including the correction of significant known deficiencies, has been completed.
- In many cases it may be prudent to defer work until the post-delivery period before the vessel is transferred to the fleet, for example for financial or workload reasons.

In addition, the Navy's fixed-price shipbuilding contracts that we reviewed included the Navy's Delivery of Completed Vessel clause, which requires the shipbuilder, before the ship is delivered to the Navy, to satisfactorily correct all contractor responsible deficiencies as necessary to avoid an adverse effect on the operational capability of the vessel.[15]

Different units in the Navy disagree over when ships should be free from deficiencies. The Office of the Chief of Naval Operations, the authors of the policy, state that the policy is to accept delivery of a vessel from the shipbuilder that is free of deficiencies, especially all contractor-responsible deficiencies. However, program office and SUPSHIP officials, as well as officials from other Navy organizations, stated that it is standard practice for the Navy to accept delivery of a ship with numerous unresolved deficiencies and/or incomplete work. Navy program officials point to the part of the policy that states that the vessel should be fully mission capable by the Obligation and Work Limiting Date—the time full financial responsibility for the ship is transferred to the operational fleet—

---

[15]The Delivery on Completed Vessel clause also requires that prior to commencing acceptance trials the contractor has: (1) satisfactorily carried out builder's trials for which the contractor is responsible, (2) corrected all shipbuilder-responsible deficiencies discovered before completion of the builder's sea trials, unless otherwise agreed to by the contracting officer in writing; and, (3) corrected all shipbuilder-responsible deficiencies discovered after completion of the builder's sea trials which are determined by the contracting officer to be necessary to avoid an adverse effect on the operational capability of the ship.

and this is their quality goal. Thus, the Navy has routinely deferred correcting deficiencies with the intention of correcting these items during the post-delivery period, as shown in appendixes III through VI.[16] In fact, for some, such as those in the DDG 51 class, the bulk of deficiencies are addressed during the first four months following delivery to the Navy during the final outfitting period. This is the time when the crew boards the ship and begins testing and training prior to the ship being deployed on a mission. Several NAVSEA officials stated that addressing deficiencies during the post-delivery period can interfere with crew training, final outfitting, and testing of the vessel while also affecting the quality of the work being performed.

Further, while some Navy officials told us that transferring problems to the fleet is rare, the transfer of major problems to the fleet in varying degrees of severity occurred on LPD 17-21, LHD 8, and DDG 103, requiring the use of operations and maintenance funds to correct the defects. Navy operations officials told us that following the problems with LPD 17 and LPD 18 that were transferred to the fleet, the fleet has become more involved in ensuring that it receives a quality vessel. They noted that the fleet now has the ability to provide input at key points during the acquisition process on whether identified problems on a vessel have been adequately addressed.

Navy Has Implemented Some, but Not All, Quality Improvement Measures

In 2007, recognizing the widespread quality problems in new construction ships, the Commander of NAVSEA began to examine the quantity of SUPSHIP's quality assurance inspectors in a few key locations to determine what resources were needed to improve quality. Following this workforce assessment, between fiscal years 2009 and 2012, the Navy hired new staff and reallocated funding for engineering, acquisition management, and quality assurance personnel at those SUPSHIP commands with the greatest risks to quality and in order to keep up with the growth of shipbuilding programs.

In 2009, the Back to Basics effort was initiated. This effort identified several quality assurance related goals and developed a means to help SUPSHIP better communicate to the program offices the role of quality

---

[16]Appendixes III-VI provide data on the closing of deficiencies following delivery for selected surface ship classes where multiple ships were delivered to the Navy.

assurance and the purpose of quality oversight. In addition, NAVSEA standardized many of the operating procedures across all SUPSHIP locations. Another focus of Back to Basics was improving SUPSHIP's oversight of critical hull, mechanical, and electrical shipbuilding processes such as welding, painting, and cabling by standardizing and improving its use of metrics to assess shipbuilder performance in these areas. For example, on a quarterly basis, the SUPSHIP commands report to NAVSEA leadership on the extent to which the shipbuilders are meeting SUPSHIP's quality goals as compared with previous periods. These quarterly reports provide NAVSEA leadership with insight into the reasons behind any increases in quality problems.

The Back to Basics initiative prompted at least two SUPSHIP locations to use a process called "pulse audits" where SUPSHIP and shipbuilder quality inspectors conduct an inspection together to ensure that their inspections are consistent. Also, some SUPSHIP locations have regular meetings with quality inspectors from the shipbuilder to compare quality inspection results and metrics, and discuss any discrepancies between the results of their inspections. As a result, SUPSHIP and shipbuilder officials reported they now have a greater understanding of each other's quality assurance processes.

In addition, in June 2010, the Back to Basics team developed a quality performance standard that set forth common quality requirements to be included in shipbuilding contracts, which was subsequently published as a NAVSEA technical publication. The Quality Performance Standard for Construction of Naval Vessels provides standard contract language that, among other things, would require shipbuilders to

- develop and submit a quality assurance plan for the government's approval;
- conduct a review to identify special controls, processes, equipment, and skills required for assuring product quality;
- ensure that drawings are reviewed for adequacy and completeness before use;
- have a quality system that ensures that work is inspected and/or tested at points necessary to ensure conformance with contract requirements;
- respond to corrective action requests within 21 days (7 days for safety issues) and indicate when corrective action will be completed;
- maintain and use cost data on prevention and detection of defects and failure costs (such as scrap, rework, and repairs);

- provide the government electronic access to quality, accuracy control, and manufacturing process data; and
- use results-oriented indicators to demonstrate quality program effectiveness.

Although the standard was developed in 2010, according to officials who wrote it, as of September 2013 none of the Navy's shipbuilding programs had incorporated this quality performance standard into their shipbuilding contracts. Further, in a May 2013 meeting, senior NAVSEA leadership told us they were unaware that a quality performance standard had been developed, noting that quality clauses are already included in the Navy's shipbuilding contracts. According to officials from SUPSHIP and the SUPSHIP Management Group, the quality standard was developed because of inconsistencies in quality requirements included in shipbuilding contracts that decreased the Navy's ability to effectively conduct oversight. For example, we reviewed two fixed-price-incentive shipbuilding contracts awarded in fiscal year 2011 that contain very different quality requirements. On one contract for a relatively mature ship class, the quality clause includes production process control, data sharing, and the use of results-oriented metrics to demonstrate quality program effectiveness. On another contract for a newer ship class, the quality clause simply requires that the shipbuilder develop, implement, and maintain a quality assurance plan covering certain aspects of shipbuilding.

Further, SUPSHIP officials cited one recent contract that did not include provisions for SUPSHIP to review the shipbuilder's work procedures. As a result, the builder was reluctant to provide this information as it was not contractually required, limiting SUPSHIP's ability to discover potential problems. SUPSHIP officials noted that, under current contracts, the range of data provided may not be sufficient for them to do their work. For example, officials noted that one fixed-price-incentive contract stated that "processes or indicators (internal design changes, production rework, etc.) to be monitored and reported shall be agreed to by the Program Office and shall be identified in the management plan(s);" without going into any additional detail about the specific types of data or the frequency with which data was to be provided.

Views regarding the success of Back to Basics are mixed. NAVSEA leadership views it as a success, noting that maintaining the improvements made over the last few years will be critical as budgets shrink and the shipbuilding portfolio shifts into more steady-state production. They point to the LPD 17 and T-AKE programs as evidence of the benefits resulting from the quality assurance staffing increases. However, others within the Navy believe that quality improvements on some shipbuilding programs, such as the T-AKE program, were largely independent of the initiative.

Commercial Firms Resolve Quality Deficiencies before Delivery, with Some Practices Potentially Informative for Navy in Spite of Different Environment

The environment in which leading commercial ship buyers and builders operate differs in substantial ways from the Navy's. Key differences include the level of competition, different incentives at play, and the timing of ship deliveries to the end user. Nevertheless, some commercial practices supporting delivery of ships with a minimum number of deficiencies may be useful for the Navy. These practices include

- a focus on resolving deficiencies before ship delivery,
- contracting approaches that place the cost risk associated with addressing quality problems on the shipbuilder and incentivize prompt resolution of problems, and
- an oversight process with clear lines of accountability and an emphasis on observing in-process work.

Environment and Key Incentives Differ between Commercial and Navy Shipbuilding

The commercial shipyards and ship buyers we visited build and buy ships that are highly complex and densely outfitted. These ships include floating production storage and offloading (FPSO) vessels, which collect, process, and store oil from undersea oil fields; large cruise ships, some of which are comparable to the size of an aircraft carrier and can accommodate over 5,000 passengers; liquefied natural gas carriers; and offshore drilling ships, which in some instances can sit unanchored and drill for oil in water depths of over 10,000 feet while maintaining a fixed position. Construction can take up to three years at a cost ranging from about $600 million for a drill ship to well over $1 billion for a cruise ship or FPSO. In many cases, these ships incorporate technological advances that are vital to improving business operations. For example, for enhancing operational and commercial efficiencies, the new generation liquefied natural gas carriers developed a range of techniques from reliquefaction of the boil off gas to its utilization as fuel for engines for propulsion. Key characteristics of selected commercial ships and offshore structures included in our review are presented in appendix VIII.

Commercial shipbuilders, particularly those in the oil and gas industry, operate in a robust, competitive environment, as opposed to the U.S. Navy's limited shipbuilding industrial base, where sole source contracts may be awarded in order to sustain workloads and the solvency of the companies involved. This environment provides commercial buyers with additional leverage to expect quality at delivery, as they can go elsewhere if they are not satisfied with the end product. One oil and gas company reported that there are as many as a dozen shipbuilders from which they can solicit proposals at any one time. As a result, commercial shipbuilders put a premium on reputation. They do not want to risk their credibility with buyers if the ship is not delivered by the contracted delivery date with the buyer's expected level of quality. These factors create additional pressure on the shipbuilder to ensure that outstanding deficiencies are resolved in a timely manner. In contrast, the Navy has fewer choices of shipbuilders and has an interest in sustaining these shipbuilders despite shortfalls in performance.

In addition, commercial buyers and builders operate in an environment where both parties seek to maximize profits. A delay in delivery has significant profit impacts to both the buyer and shipbuilder. For example, it is common for a drill ship to be leased to an oil and gas company early during the ship's construction process, and both the ship buyer and the company leasing the vessel rely on the ship to be at its drill site by the contracted date to begin operations. Any delay in meeting this schedule can not only cause the ship buyer to lose revenue—which for some drill ships can amount to over $600,000 per day—but also may require the buyer to pay predetermined sums to the company leasing the drill ship for lost work days. Also, newly constructed cruise ships are expected to start generating revenue weeks if not days after being delivered. For example, Royal Caribbean officials told us that they had a full cruise 3 days after taking delivery of the *Celebrity Solstice* in October 2008. The monetary risks faced by the ship buyer for late delivery or acquiring a ship that does not meet key performance requirements—such as fuel consumption—are also passed along to the shipbuilder in the form of liquidated damages that can potentially cost the shipbuilder tens of millions of dollars.[17]

Celebrity Solstice

Source: Royal Caribbean Cruises Ltd.

---

[17]Liquidated damages are amounts contractually stipulated as a reasonable estimation of actual damages to be recovered by one party if the other party breaches.

Leading Commercial Ship Buyers Focus on Taking Delivery of Ships Meeting Quality Expectations

Throughout the construction process, the ship buyer's oversight team, the shipbuilders' quality personnel, and classification society personnel routinely identify deficiencies such as design errors, supplier and vendor quality issues, and problems with workmanship. Commercial ship buyers we met with expect that identified problems will be corrected prior to delivery of the ship. We found this to be the case for all types of ships included in our assessment of commercial practices, whether a lead ship (i.e., the first ship built according to a new design) or a ship built from a proven design. Unresolved issues that affect the safety, seaworthiness, or operability of the ship would be reason for the ship buyer to not accept delivery until such items are corrected. For the generally minor deficiencies that have not been corrected by the ship's delivery date, the buyer and shipbuilder may enter into a formal agreement outlining specific actions that the builder will take to ensure correction of the outstanding issues in the prescribed time.

There is a fair amount of subjectivity as to what constitutes a major or minor deficiency that largely depends on the ship's intended use. While each ship-buying company may take a slightly different view of what constitutes a major or minor deficiency, minor deficiencies are generally those items that do not have an effect on the mission, operability, or safety of the vessel and are not indicative of problems with the builder's production processes. Major deficiencies can be viewed as problems with the shipbuilder's production processes that limit the builder's ability to meet ship specifications, or those deficiencies that could have an adverse effect on the mission, operability, or safety of the vessel if not resolved. We found that commercial ship buyer definitions for major and minor deficiencies do not necessarily align with the definitions used by the Navy. For example, in the cruise industry, where aesthetics and the customer experience are critical factors, a major deficiency may be an issue such as higher than anticipated engine vibration or elevated noise levels. Typical minor deficiencies include cosmetic defects such as scratches on windows, paint, and furniture. For oil and gas ships that are expected to endure harsh environments, common major outstanding deficiencies at the time of delivery could involve equipment that has not yet been installed or equipment that requires additional calibration. Typical minor deficiencies might include missing signage or technical manuals.

A drill ship for Noble Corporation, the *Noble Don Taylor*, illustrates the process for correcting deficiencies leading up to delivery of commercial ships. In this case, the shipbuilder reduced the number of corrective items, totaling over 15,000 throughout construction, to around 3,800 by

Noble Corporation's *Noble Don Taylor* dynamically positioned drill ship

Source: Noble Corporation.

the time sea trials were scheduled to occur. At the time of ship delivery, the number of unresolved corrective actions was down to just over 59 items, which the shipbuilder agreed to correct no later than three months following the date of delivery. One day following ship delivery, this number dropped to 37 items. These items included minor deficiencies such as incorrect labels and missing manufacturer documentation for equipment, and in some instances, more significant corrective actions including replacement of equipment which measures the weight and torque of the drill that did not have the correct calibration.

Additional examples depicting the extent to which quality problems identified by the ship buyer are resolved prior to key delivery milestones are provided in table 1.

Table 1: Unresolved Deficiencies for Select Commercial Ships at Key Delivery Milestones

Ship name (type)	Delivery date	Prior to sea trials		After sea trials		At ship delivery	
		Open minor deficiencies	Open major deficiencies	Open minor deficiencies	Open major deficiencies	Open minor deficiencies	Open major deficiencies
Noble Don Taylor (drill ship)	April 2013	3,803	7	1,839	6	37	22
Seadrill Ltd. West Auriga (drill ship)	April 2013	387	78	455	105	50	0
Chevron Big Foot (tension leg platform production facility – hull structure only)[a]	December 2012	436	89	16	26	[a]	[a]
Ensco DS 6 (drill ship)	January 2012	~100	0	<100	0	4	0
Celebrity Cruises, Inc. (subsidiary of Royal Caribbean Cruises, LTD.) *Reflection* (cruise ship)	October 2012	9,110	30	8,100	25	680	20
Star Deep Water Petroleum, LTD (a Chevron-affiliated company) *Agbami* – Floating Production, Storage and Offloading vessel (FPSO)	June 2008	2,051	150	164	10	15	0

Source: GAO analysis of industry-provided data.

[a]This project used a unit rate contract where the shipbuilder is paid a specific rate for performance of the work that is proportional to the volume of work needed to complete the project. The contractor that is integrating the production facility onto the hull of the platform, rather than the shipyard, will address the open deficiencies. Therefore the ship buyer could not provide us with the data.

The commercial ships reviewed were delivered with considerably fewer defects than is common with Navy ships, even with the recent improvements realized by the Navy. With the exception of the Celebrity cruise ship where there were a large number of minor (often cosmetic) uncorrected deficiencies at the time of delivery, the number of total deficiencies ranged from 4 to 59 for the commercial ships reviewed. For the Navy, recent T-AKE class ships, the Joint High Speed Vessel, and the Mobile Landing Platform were comparable to the numbers of outstanding deficiencies found on commercial ships.

Commercial Ship Buyers Put More Risk on Shipbuilders through Choice of Contract Type and Payment Structure

The Navy and commercial ship buyers agree that responsibility for quality must be put on the shipbuilders, as they are in the best position to ensure quality. However, the commercial buyers we spoke with structure their contracts to ensure that the shipbuilder absorbs the cost risks associated with quality problems. For example, they require delivery of a ship at an expected quality level for a firm-fixed-price and delay a majority of payment until the expectation is met. The Navy shares more of the cost risk associated with delivery of a quality product with its shipbuilders through cost-reimbursement[18] and fixed-price-incentive[19] contracts. The Navy also makes regular progress payments throughout construction so that the bulk of payment has already been made by delivery.

---

[18]The Federal Acquisition Regulation (FAR) authorizes use of a cost reimbursement contract when circumstances do not allow the agency to define its requirements sufficiently to allow for a fixed-price type of contract or uncertainties involved in contract performance do not permit costs to be estimated with sufficient accuracy to use any type of fixed-price contract. When using this contract type the government pays for all allowable incurred costs to the extent prescribed in the contract.

[19]The FAR authorizes use of fixed-price-incentive contracts when a firm fixed-price contract is not suitable; the nature of the supplies or services being acquired and other circumstances of the acquisition are such that the contractor's assumption of a degree of cost responsibility will provide a positive profit incentive for effective cost control and performance. If the contract also includes incentives on technical performance and/or delivery, the performance requirements provide a reasonable opportunity for the incentives to have a meaningful impact on the contractor's management of the work. This contract type provides that the government and the contractor generally share costs—pursuant to a formula—above the target cost and below the ceiling price.

Commercial Ship Buyers Use Firm Fixed-Price Contracts to Put Cost Risk of Poor Quality on the Shipbuilder

Firm fixed-price contracts used in commercial shipbuilding—even for lead ships—put more of the cost risks associated with quality on the shipbuilder than cost-reimbursement and fixed-price-incentive contracts which are commonly used by the Navy. Under a firm-fixed-price contract, the shipbuilder takes on the full cost of any quality problems that result in rework. As many quality problems require rework to existing blocks or compartments and can thus erode the shipbuilder's profit that is included in the firm-fixed-price, there is a greater incentive to minimize production deficiencies throughout construction.

Similar to commercial ship buyers, the Navy has made some limited use of firm-fixed-price contracts to purchase ships included in our review, and in those cases the contractor has taken on more cost risk associated with any quality problems. Of the 11 shipbuilding programs we reviewed, three (DDG 51, T-AKE, and T-AGM 25) used firm-fixed-price contracts.[20] For example, starting with the 10th ship in the T-AKE ship class, the Navy successfully moved to a firm fixed-price contract for the remaining 5 ships. Whereas some of the earlier T-AKE ships exceeded the contracted target price, the ships constructed under firm-fixed-price contracts continued to maintain good quality. T-AGM 25 was purchased using a firm-fixed-price contracting arrangement from the outset, but in this case the project experienced quality problems and delays. Although the shipbuilding project did not perform as expected, the Navy's exposure to cost overruns resulting from quality problems was mitigated.

Under a cost-reimbursement contract, the cost risks associated with poor quality remain with the Navy because the government pays for all allowable costs of construction, including any rework, although lower costs may be incentivized by the use of award or incentive fees. The Navy has used cost-reimbursable contracts on lead ships due to concerns that the level of uncertainty and risk common on Navy programs make fixed-price contracts too costly. For example, one NAVSEA directorate stated that some Navy shipbuilding programs would likely be deemed unaffordable under a fixed-price contract due to the shipbuilders' need to include in the price the risk of uncertainty associated with new construction methods, new technologies, and new designs. However, the Navy generally moves more mature ship programs to fixed-price-incentive

---

[20]In late 2011, DDG 108, DDG 109, DDG 111, and DDG 112 transitioned to firm-fixed-price contract line items from fixed-price-incentive contract line items. At the time only DDG 112 was still under construction.

contracts, and Navy officials have stated that the cost sharing provisions in this type of contract incentivize quality. Under a fixed-price-incentive type contract, the contract is awarded for a target cost. The Navy and the shipbuilder share both cost savings and cost overruns below or above the target cost (referred to as the "share line"), pursuant to a formula, until the ceiling price is reached. Navy officials have stated that they see this type of contract as an incentive to quality because the shipbuilders will receive more profit if they construct the ship efficiently and deliver it below the target cost. Appendix IX further illustrates how cost risks pertaining to quality are allocated under the different contract types.

Commercial Shipbuilding Payment Terms Put More Pressure on Shipbuilder to Deliver Complete Ship at Expected Quality Level

In the commercial world, ship buyers use payment terms as leverage to ensure that the shipbuilder delivers a ship to the expected level of quality. Payments are generally made at milestones negotiated with the shipbuilder, such as contract signing, steel cutting, and keel laying. The bulk of the payment, sometimes 60 to 80 percent, is made only on delivery of a ship that meets expected quality and performance levels. The buyers we met with alter payment terms based on the quality of the shipbuilder and also use the payment terms to incentivize the builder to fix any outstanding deficiencies prior to making the last payment. For example, one construction manager stated that his company normally makes equal payments to shipbuilders at five different milestones, so that 20 percent of the ship cost remains to be paid at delivery, but the company would likely increase the percentage of the overall payment outstanding at delivery with a lesser quality shipbuilder. Another ship buyer said that his company normally pays 60 to 70 percent of contract price at delivery, but would not make final payment if the ship had major outstanding quality issues. Two other ship buyers told us they make milestone payments during construction, but generally retain 5 to 10 percent of the payment as a means to ensure that the builder addresses deficiencies before delivery. Those buyers also said they can retain these funds at delivery to ensure prompt resolution of any unresolved deficiencies. These practices create a strong financial incentive for the builder to quickly complete work and clear any outstanding quality defects. One project manager indicated that on two recent shipbuilding projects, it was not necessary to withhold any of the payment after taking delivery of the vessels because of the small number of deficiencies.

Of the 11 fixed-price contracts we reviewed (with the exception of TAGM-25), the Navy makes periodic payments to its shipbuilders according to the progress made in construction.[21] For example, one contract allows the shipbuilder to submit payment invoices every two weeks that are based on the progress made in construction as long as the billed amount is over $5,000. While commercial ship buyers may pay the bulk of payment at delivery, this system also requires shipbuilders to finance construction and related finance costs, which are ultimately passed on to the ship buyer in the contract cost.

According to Navy contracting officials, they consider potential impacts on pricing in developing payment provisions. In the fixed-priced shipbuilding contracts we reviewed, we found that the Navy generally retains a percentage from each progress payment—anywhere up to 10 percent— that decreases as the ship is being built. Navy contracting officials told us that they will only reduce the retention to the lower percentage once outstanding problems have been cleared. The following example from a recent shipbuilding contract illustrates this process:

- Up to 25 percent of the ship's physical completion—5 percent is retained from each progress payment;
- 25 to 50 percent of the ship's physical completion—3 percent is retained from each progress payment;
- 50 to 75 percent of the ship's physical completion—1.5 percent is retained from each progress payment; and
- Once 75 percent of the ship's physical completion has been reached—1 percent is retained from each remaining progress payment.

At delivery, the Navy retains a minimum amount of the shipbuilder's payment as a performance reserve that ranges from 0.75 to 1.5 percent of the ship's contract value, and will withhold additional funds from the shipbuilder's last invoice or the amount retained during construction if there are uncorrected deficiencies or incomplete work. However, the Navy may be constrained in terms of how it can incentivize contractors since the bulk of payments are made during the course of construction rather than at delivery. As it is common for Navy ships to have many more deficiencies and incomplete work items at delivery than the commercial ships in our review, the amount retained may not sufficiently motivate the shipbuilder to correct all deficiencies. Further, there is not

---

[21]Payments made during construction of T-AGM 25 were based on the shipbuilder's achievement of certain shipbuilding milestones, such as keel laying.

specific NAVSEA guidance that addresses the extent to which retentions should be used as a means to incentivize the shipbuilder to promptly resolve outstanding deficiencies and incomplete work items at ship delivery. However, standards for internal control in the federal government identify the need for documenting policies and procedures to ensure appropriate measures are taken to address risk.[22] Program officials stated that for uncorrected deficiencies that are large in scope they will typically develop an estimated cost to complete each item. For the remaining deficiencies, the officials stated they develop an average cost that is based on the estimated cost to complete a selected sample of the deficiencies and apply that cost universally across the remaining deficiencies. In the case of LHD 8, which was delivered to the Navy in April 2009 with over 12,000 outstanding shipbuilder-responsible deficiencies, the Navy retained about 2.5 percent of the final estimated cost. Navy officials told us that some of these outstanding items are still being completed during maintenance periods.

More recently, Navy and SUPSHIP officials stated that in at least three instances they have temporarily increased the amount of the retained payments in an effort to prompt the shipbuilder to correct persistent deficiencies. SUPSHIP officials told us this approach was successful for problems they encountered with the LHA 6, DDG 51, and LPD 17 ship classes. In the case of LPD 17 class ships, the Navy withheld over $15 million in progress payments on four ships that were under construction until the shipbuilder resolved persistent problems with pipe cleanliness.

---

[22]See GAO, *Standards for Internal Control in the Federal Government*, GAO/AIMD-00-21.3.1 (Washington, D.C.: Nov. 1999).

Commercial and Navy Shipbuilding Utilize Differing Approaches to Foster Accountability and Ensure Quality

Commercial Ship Buyer Oversight Structure Creates Clear Lines of Accountability While Navy Oversight Is More Diffused

Another mechanism commercial ship buyers use to ensure quality assurance is having dedicated, trained inspection teams on site to monitor and oversee all aspects of construction. All of the commercial ship buyers we met with create clear lines of responsibility for functional areas to ensure accountability within their on-site teams, which are primarily responsible for quality during construction. Within the on-site teams of the commercial buyers we met with, responsibility for a functional area such as paint or hull and structure is consolidated under one functional area lead who reports to the buyer's overall project or construction manager on-site. The on-site project manager has overall responsibility within the buyer's company to ensure that the shipbuilder delivers the ship on time and at the expected level of quality. Quality inspectors are integrated within each functional area team. Commercial ship buyers told us that their on-site quality inspectors are expected to independently identify critical inspection areas during the course of their day-to-day inspections. We found that commercial quality inspectors use design drawings and ship specifications during their work to ensure that the items are built in accordance with the detailed design. Furthermore, these inspectors are also responsible for tracking and closing all corrective actions they identify during the course of construction and ensuring that the corrected work or work processes resolved the identified problems. Overall, commercial ship buyers place a high-level of responsibility on their inspectors to be able to identify important quality issues in their functional area and ensure that the company will take delivery of a ship that meets quality standards.

Within the Navy, SUPSHIP quality assurance departments have limited authority over the shipbuilder compared to commercial ship buyers' inspectors. SUPSHIP quality assurance teams identify and report defects found during their inspections, and can close out the deficiencies once the defects are rectified. However, deficiencies that are technical in nature, or with which the builder disagrees, are adjudicated by SUPSHIP engineering and the ship's program office and not the quality assurance department. For example, SUPSHIP's engineering department reviews and adjudicates technical issues related to design and system engineering that quality assurance teams identify during inspections. If the engineering group finds that a defect is technically acceptable, a waiver may be provided indicating that the shipbuilder does not need to correct the defect. The ship's program office is primarily responsible for successful delivery of the ship, including responsibility for cost, schedule and performance requirements. Program office officials also review certain defects identified by the SUPSHIP quality assurance teams and make the determination as to whether or not they will be corrected by the shipbuilder, provided the defect is technically acceptable.

As shown in figure 13 below, there are major departments within SUPSHIP, such as contracting, engineering, and program management that have delegated responsibilities from the respective NAVSEA level directorates or the PEOs and are able to elevate technical risks or concerns about the structure of the shipbuilding contract to those that have decision-making authority. SUPSHIP quality officials receive policy guidance from the NAVSEA Logistics, Maintenance and Industrial Operations Directorate (NAVSEA 04), but there is not a quality assurance team at the NAVSEA level to which they can raise quality related issues.

Figure 13: Simplified Organizational Chart of SUPSHIP Indicating Those Departments Having Delegated Responsibilities

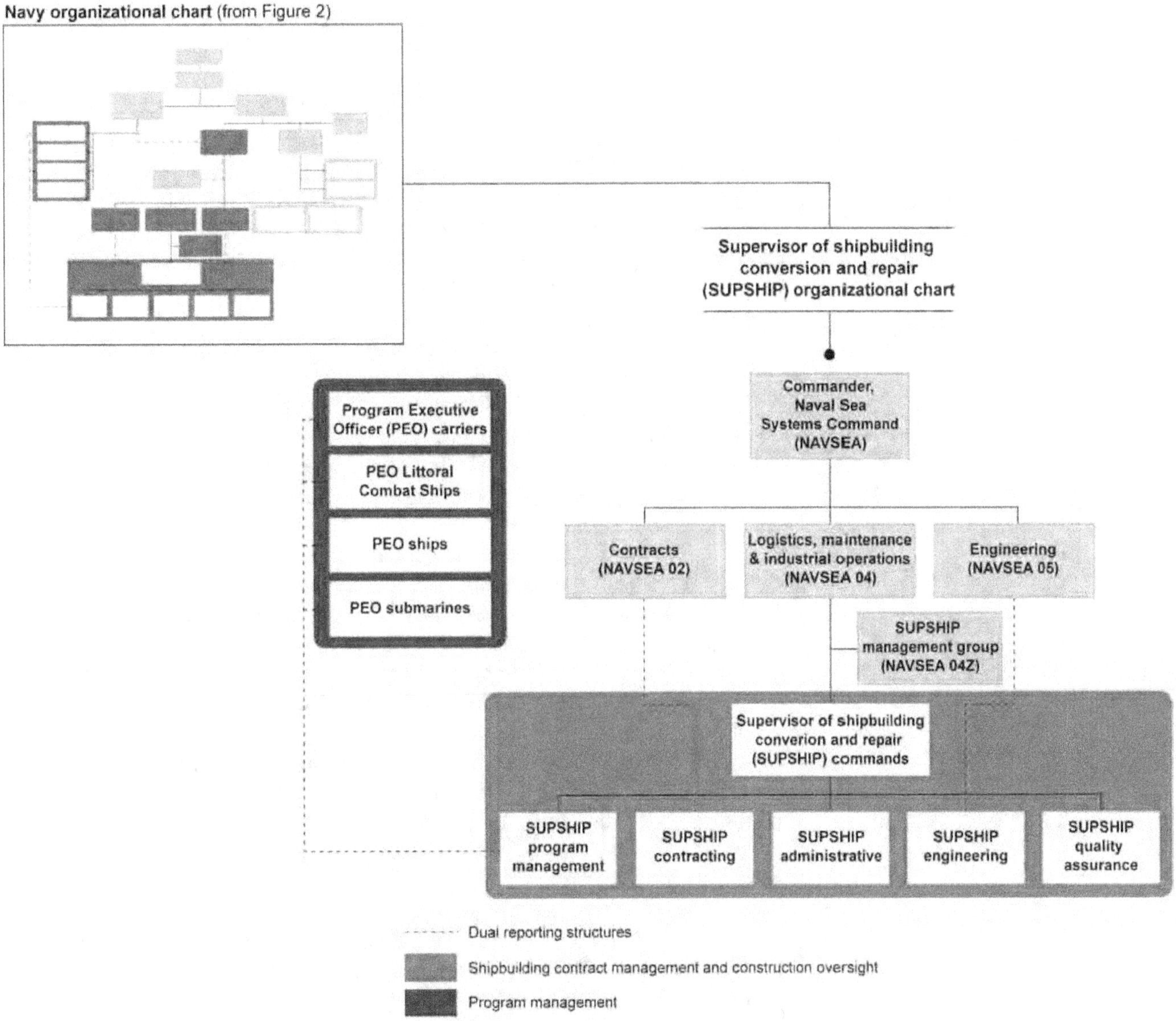

Navy organizational chart (from Figure 2)

Source: GAO analysis of Navy data.

Officials within NAVSEA 04 told us the Navy is formulating plans to reorganize the structure of the directorate, and plans include establishing a centralized quality team. Although the roles, responsibilities, and authorities of the quality team are not yet defined, the officials expect that the team would provide support to SUPSHIP quality assurance departments in helping to ensure that matters related to quality are given sufficient attention at the NAVSEA level. Increasing the emphasis on quality may help contribute to the goal of delivering ships that are defect-free, or nearly defect-free, as called for in Navy policy and demonstrated in commercial shipbuilding.

Commercial Ship Buyers Align Quality Inspections with Shipbuilder Plans While Navy Has Multiple Inspection Plans, Fewer In-Process Inspections

Prior to construction, the commercial ship buyers and shipbuilders we met with negotiate to one common understanding of quality inspections through an agreed-upon quality inspection plan.[23] The plan identifies (1) all formal inspection points during the construction process; (2) who attends and approves the inspections; and (3) criteria on how the inspections will be carried out. One ship buyer noted that establishing the quality inspection plan in conjunction with the shipbuilder and ensuring that all parties agree to, and are aware of, the key drivers that affect quality is of the utmost importance in ensuring the ship is built and delivered at the expected level of quality. According to company officials, the shipbuilder is contractually required to notify the buyer of any formal inspection points to provide the buyer an opportunity to inspect a product or process at a designated point of production.

Buyer representatives, including on-site teams and headquarter-level officials, review the builder's quality inspection plan and may ask for additional inspections and hold points based on ship design, criticality of the system, and previous experiences of the buyer. For example, one ship buyer reported experiencing significant failure rates during pressure testing of piping systems on a drill rig, and decided to incorporate additional inspection points at the joints where pipes are welded together on future drill ship projects. In another instance, a ship buyer representative told us his company solicits input on the quality inspection plan from company personnel that operate similar types of vessels, which he noted provides valuable information on the types of quality issues observed from an operator's perspective. The quality inspection plan is a key tool in ensuring quality as it enables consistency in inspections by focusing the ship buyer and builder on the same inspection items using the same criteria. Figure 14 further describes actions taken by one commercial firm, Chevron's Project Resources Company, to improve quality.

---

[23]Leading commercial ship buyers and shipbuilders in oil and gas, cruise and shipping industries referred to these plans by different terms, such as an inspection and test plan or yard quality standard.

Figure 14: Actions Taken by a Commercial Firm to Improve Quality

Chevron Corporation's Big Foot tension leg platform undergoing construction; Ingleside, Texas.

Chevron Project Resources Company

When Chevron's Project Resources Company (PRC), which manages Chevron's major capital projects such as deep-sea and offshore oil and gas exploration and production projects, noticed an increase in quality issues, it took on a stronger role in ensuring quality by incorporating quality assurance personnel into their project team structure—a structure that previously relied more on contractor oversight and the builder's quality systems. PRC's quality inspectors are tasked with auditing and conducting surveillance of the builder's and major suppliers' quality systems and work processes. In addition, the company established a centralized quality group to provide functional support to project-level quality personnel and act as a quality advocate, so that project issues affecting quality may be elevated to a management level if necessary. From a contracting perspective, the centralized quality group created standardized contract language for quality that is used on projects managed by PRC. The project-level quality managers play a role in the contracting process in terms of tailoring the standardized quality clauses to meet the specific needs of the project and working with the builder's quality department to ensure quality requirements are well understood. PRC's team lead for quality management said that, to be effective, these quality improvement efforts required the full support of the company's leadership, a change in corporate culture, and an overall acceptance that while there is a cost to quality, the benefits are worth the costs.

Source: Chevron Project Resources Company Data.

Inspectors for commercial ship buyers enforce quality requirements, in part, by attending all formal inspections, according to almost all of the commercial ship buyers in our review (seven of nine companies). For example, one ship buyer we met with reported having up to 80 inspections in a day for the team of about 14 inspectors. These inspectors use design drawings and review the ship specification to ensure that the compartment or block is built in accordance with requirements.

Along with the formal inspections, commercial ship buyers consistently cited "roaming patrols" as central to their oversight process. Inspectors regularly patrol the shipyard, where they observe the shipyard's in-process work. All of the buyers emphasized the importance of these patrols as providing assurance that shipbuilders are adhering to their work processes even when a formal inspection is not scheduled. These patrols facilitate the early recognition of quality problems, which are typically less expensive and time consuming to correct than later in the construction process. Some officials told us that these impromptu patrols can be particularly effective in yards with more quality issues. The percentage of inspectors' time allocated to these roaming patrols can vary depending on the stage of construction—but can exceed 50 percent over the course of a ship's construction—with a greater proportion of time allocated during the earlier stages of construction when there are not as many formal inspections.

In contrast to commercial shipbuilding, where buyer and builder inspection activities are aligned through one common inspection plan, Navy shipbuilding involves layers of oversight and quality inspections that are resource intensive and not necessarily aligned with shipbuilders' inspections. In Navy shipbuilding, NAVSEA officials told us formal inspection points that relate to quality are identified in multiple ways including Navy technical documents, inspection proposals from the shipbuilder, or the ship's technical specifications. NAVSEA's engineering directorate reviews and approves the shipbuilder's quality-related test and inspection documents. Other formal test and inspection points, such as those for equipment and system installations, are contained in separate test plans that the shipbuilder develops and SUPSHIP engineering reviews. In addition to attending formal inspections, SUPSHIP's quality assurance department independently develops its own surveillance plans, and these surveillance plans are revised several times a year.[24]

Unlike inspectors for commercial ship buyers, SUPSHIP inspectors do not attend all formal inspections identified in the shipbuilding contract. SUPSHIP quality managers determine which inspections their inspectors attend—generally based on priority or potential problem areas—but it is understood that inspectors will not attend all call-outs, in part due to staffing levels at the SUPSHIP locations. NAVSEA and SUPSHIP officials noted that the unpredictability of which inspections will be attended by SUPSHIP helps ensure the shipbuilder maintains focus on all aspects of production.

SUPSHIP officials described their oversight approach in very different terms than commercial ship buyers. SUPSHIP surveillance plans set forth goals that focus on collecting numbers of observations. SUPSHIP quality assurance teams in the locations we visited stated that they generally focus most of their inspection efforts, in terms of observations conducted,

---

[24]Nuclear submarines and aircraft carriers are also subject to additional oversight and inspection by NAVSEA 08 officials, who are responsible for nuclear propulsion systems. Navy submarines are subject to additional specialized inspections through its Submarine Safety program. Inspections conducted through this program, as well as audits and observations made by NAVSEA's Nuclear Propulsion Directorate of all shipyard activities, can also identify broader quality issues that affect construction. For example, Newport News Shipbuilding experienced issues with welders using incorrect filler material on Virginia Class Submarines. While Newport News was already working on the issue, audits by NAVSEA 08 identified it as a systemic problem, elevating the severity of the problem, according to officials. The Navy and the shipbuilder subsequently led a thorough review of weld filler materials used in potentially affected vessels.

on performing planned inspections identified in shipbuilding contracts and SUPSHIP surveillance plans, and less effort conducting random inspections of in-process work (similar to the roaming patrols used by commercial buyers' inspectors). The main inspection activity carried out by SUPSHIP quality inspectors, as measured by the number of observations, are product verification inspections. These are inspections of end products such as fabricated blocks, installed equipment, and completed compartments to ensure that the work conforms to the contract specifications. SUPSHIP's Gulf Coast and Bath locations reported spending 64 percent and 60 percent, respectively, of their inspection efforts on product verification inspections, while Groton and Newport News spent less time—39 percent and 35 percent, respectively.

As part of SUPSHIPs' surveillance plan for a shipyard, quality inspectors also observe work being performed by production workers—work that is in process—for compliance with the builders' procedures and technical specifications. Similar to commercial ship buyers, SUPSHIP officials stated it is important to identify, and remedy, any potential quality issues early in the construction process. Most SUPSHIP locations reported spending about 30 percent of their inspection efforts on in-process evaluations. These evaluations are planned in advance and may last a few hours to several days. SUPSHIP officials have reported that they are putting more effort into in-process inspection activities-rather than just inspecting end products For example, one SUPSHIP location has established a goal of having 70 percent of their inspectors' observations related to in-process work. SUPSHIP officials also told us that their inspectors conduct some general surveillance or random inspections, but it is unclear how much of their effort is spent on these activities as they are not recorded as such.

Also in contrast to commercial shipbuilding practice, not all SUPSHIP locations use design drawings while conducting inspections. Instead, inspectors use pre-developed checklists and ship technical specifications to perform inspections. The use of design drawings during inspections helps to ensure that work is being produced in accordance with the approved design and that the builder's workers are using the correct version of the design. For example, ABS officials told us that during construction of the Littoral Combat Ship, ABS found in a number of instances that the production drawings used to build the ship were different from the approved design. In some cases the production drawings identified different sizes of pipes and flanges, or depicted piping arrangements that were not included in the approved design, but such issues generally went unnoticed by the SUPSHIP inspectors because they did not compare the design drawings to the work performed. Quality officials at two SUPSHIP locations stated that their inspectors have been trained and use the design drawings during inspections, and officials from both locations view this as an important tool for ensuring quality.[25] Officials at one of these SUPSHIP locations said they have long realized the benefits of using design drawings during the course of their quality inspectors' work and ensure the inspectors are trained to be able to read design drawings. At the other location, officials stated they just recently started having their quality inspectors use the design drawings when conducting quality inspections, which they attribute as being a good practice they observed from ABS.

Commercial Shipbuilders' Quality Management Systems Enforce Accountability for Quality Down to the Worker Level

No. 3 Dry dock at HHI, Ulsan Shipyard, South Korea

Source: Hyundai Heavy Industries (HHI).

Commercial shipbuilders create an environment of accountability for quality by implementing systems to track quality problems down to the supervisor and individual worker level. Systems used by shipbuilders included complex enterprise resource management systems that track workers assigned to specific work packages or assignments, as well as simple systems such as requiring production workers to sign their work (on the compartment itself or related paperwork) with a unique identifier. For example, one shipbuilder we visited conducts non-destructive tests on welds as dictated in the quality inspection plan developed with the ship buyer. Each test record includes information on the welder who performed the work and the outcome of the testing. This allows the shipbuilder to identify welders producing defective work. Furthermore, the shipbuilder uses the test data to rate welder performance across the yard as part of its regular performance appraisal system. This same system allows the shipbuilder to track performance of supervisors and individual workers in terms of producing quality products and minimizing rework.

Most Navy shipbuilding contractors we met with (five of eight shipyards) reported that they have historically had difficulties identifying when and where in the production process specific quality problems occurred, as work was not always tracked at the supervisor or individual worker level. This has been a major challenge that they have been trying to address in recent years. The shipbuilders agree that quality problems are generally the result of a breakdown with the execution of their quality management

[25]Officials at one other SUPSHIP location indicated their quality inspectors use the builder's production drawings when conducting inspections.

plans rather than problems with the plans themselves.[26] Most of the Navy contractor shipyards we visited reported having made progress on this front, and shipbuilder quality representatives told us they have been able to improve the detection of quality problems earlier in the production process and hold front-line supervisors accountable for the quality of the work they oversee. For example, quality officials at one shipbuilder told us that their quality personnel are now focusing more on conducting in-process inspections to identify process-related problems occurring within a specific trade or work crew, as opposed to inspecting completed work products and then trying to locate the specific source of the problem within the broader production process. In another example, a shipbuilder has created quality advocates within the various tradecrafts that augment the builder's quality assurance department by assisting with day-to-day quality activities, such as conducting inspections and providing training, as well as representing production workers in yard-wide quality improvement efforts. Further, there are signs that builders are starting to hold their workforce accountable for quality issues. For example, a quality official at one shipyard we visited told us that his inspectors now routinely collect quality and defect data at the production supervisor level and develop a report of where each supervisor ranks as compared to the peer group. These reports are posted throughout the production facilities and are visible to all employees. In some rare instances, the quality official reported that his company instituted disciplinary actions for supervisors that repeatedly allowed poor quality work products to proceed to the next stage of production.

In addition, Navy shipbuilding contractors reported that quality at some of the shipyards has been affected by high attrition rates, making it difficult to maintain a qualified workforce. One shipbuilder representative told us that his company is recruiting new technical graduates from other parts of the country to fulfill their production staff needs. Another shipbuilder representative told us that his company has had quality problems related to inexperienced labor. The need to put new staff in place to meet work demands puts pressure on the builders to expedite hiring and training. According to one shipbuilder, without a rigorous hiring and training program, under-qualified workers could be performing the work, leading to higher incidences of quality issues. Although the four international

---

[26]We reviewed the quality assurance plans and policies of the eight Navy shipbuilding contractors and found them to be consistent with ISO 9000 quality management standards.

commercial shipbuilders we visited did not report having similar labor problems, we were told high turnover of the labor force is a problem at other commercial yards.

Classification Societies Play a Role in Commercial and Navy Shipbuilding

In commercial shipbuilding, classification societies are an integral part of design and construction processes. All of the commercial ship buyers we met with pointed out that the role of the classification society is to ensure their ships are built in accordance with the designated classification society's rules and requirements and that it is the buyers' responsibility to ensure that shipbuilders are building ships in accordance with the buyer's requirements. Further, commercial ship buyers realize that adhering to the rules and regulations of a classification society will ensure that a new construction ship only meets the quality and safety requirements stipulated in the applicable rules.

During the contracting phase, the designated classification society's applicable rules and regulations, as well as statutory requirements (such as those pertaining to safety of life issues or marine environmental protection), are generally incorporated into the shipbuilding contract. The classification society also plays a role during the design of commercial ships, as its engineers review and approve key structural design drawings to ensure the design complies with classification society rules. These engineers also review and approve key design drawings to verify compliance with any applicable statutory requirements, if so authorized by the country where the vessel will be registered. The buyers we met with had high confidence in the classification society's engineering review of the ship design and viewed this expertise as a core competency. In some instances, commercial ship buyers noted that they contract with the classification societies for engineering services when developing and testing new technologies. For example, officials from Royal Caribbean told us they sought technical assistance from the classification society Det Norske Veritas during the development and implementation of a pilot program that tested advanced engine exhaust cleaning technologies in two of its ships.[27] Figure 15 below provides additional detail on how one commercial shipbuilding project sought technical assistance from classification societies to reduce potential risks to quality.

---

[27]The advanced technologies have been installed and tested on Royal Caribbean's *Independence of the Seas* and *Liberty of the Seas* cruise ships.

Figure 15: Example of Classification Society Technical Assistance

Q-Max Liquefied Natural Gas Carrier.

ExxonMobil and Qatar Petroleum Q-Max Liquid Natural Gas (LNG) Carriers

Project: Fabrication of Q-Max LNG carrier vessels that are designed to transport up to 80 percent more cargo than traditional LNG ships with a reduction of transportation costs of 20 to 30 percent.

Undertaking a very large ship acquisition project, Exxon Mobil and its partner, Qatar Petroleum, developed two new categories of LNG carriers. They then contracted with 3 leading shipbuilders for detailed design and construction of a number of each type of carrier including a total of 14 Q-Max ships, which are currently the world's largest class of LNG carriers. During the detailed design phase of the project, each of the shipbuilders worked with the classification societies (including ABS, Det Norske Veritas and Lloyd's Register) to conduct computer modeling and simulation analysis to ensure the structural integrity of the ships was sufficient to accommodate an anticipated 40 year service life. Also during this time, project designers and engineers from Exxon Mobil and Qatar Petroleum, along with technical experts from the classification societies, conducted their own analysis to model and test the effects LNG motion had on the structural integrity of the storage tanks under normal operating and extreme sea conditions. Modeling and testing identified tank areas that needed strengthening. These changes were incorporated into the ships' design prior to the start of construction of the lead ship without affecting the delivery schedule. Officials from Exxon Mobil stressed that this effort not only mitigated potential risks to quality, but also kept design changes to a minimum throughout the shipbuilding program.

Source: GAO analysis of ExxonMobil data

Classification society surveyors also have a role in monitoring ship construction; however, none of the leading buyers we met with use their designated class society as a substitute for their own construction oversight and quality assurance processes. Specifically, while classification society surveyors assess whether the ship is constructed in accordance with prescribed rules and regulations, these rules may not take into account the ship buyer's own technical specification requirements. For example, the rules do not address the quality of every structure or piece of equipment installed on the ship, such as the ship buyer's mission-related equipment, but rather only what is determined to be critical to safe operation of the ship. In addition, class societies conduct technical assessments of key parts and equipment. For a wide range of materials, parts, and equipment used in the construction of a ship, such as main engines, generators, and pumps, it is generally a class society requirement that the surveyors attend inspections and witness testing conducted at the manufacturing facility prior to the equipment being shipped to the builder's shipyard to certify that the items comply with the applicable rule requirements.

ABS No Longer Provides Classification Services on Navy Surface Combatants but Continues to Play a Role in Navy Shipbuilding

After almost 10 years of ABS participation in the development and implementation of the Naval Vessel Rules for the DDG 1000 and LCS shipbuilding programs, the Navy, in late 2011, made a decision that as a cost savings measure it would no longer seek to obtain ABS class certification for surface combatants. ABS's services were initially expected to end in June 2012, but the Navy extended ABS's involvement on construction of LCS 4 for continued marine surveying and inspection services through October 2013. The original intent of class certification was to transfer what the Navy viewed as higher-volume, lower-risk hull, mechanical, and electrical design and construction oversight work to ABS, which would allow Navy engineers to focus on higher-risk areas including mission systems and military-unique aspects of a ship such as combat systems integration. However, according to Navy engineering officials, this process was more expensive than originally envisioned.

Of the three surface combatants—LCS 1 through LCS 3—that were designed, constructed, and delivered to the Navy under the auspices of the Naval Vessel Rules, none of the ships have received ABS class certification.[28] Prior to the Navy's determination to no longer contract for ABS's services, unresolved issues precluded issuance of class certificates.[29] According to ABS officials, the classification process involved a level of discipline that the Navy found difficult to integrate into the design and construction of surface combatants, and in some instances the Navy chose to accept design drawings or approve completed production work prior to ABS completing its own review and approval process. For example, the Naval Vessel Rules require that during the design engineering phase of the shipbuilding project computer analyses determining the structural integrity of the ship are to be reviewed and approved by ABS. However, the Navy allowed the shipbuilder to commence construction and deliver the lead ship (LCS 1) and begin construction on the second ship (LCS 3) before the ship designers were able to submit a structural analysis that met the ABS requirements. The analysis identified several areas on the ship's superstructure that were

---

[28]ABS did grant a temporary classification certificate to LCS 1 for the sole purpose of transporting the ship from the shipbuilder's facility to the Port of Norfolk, Virginia.

[29]The Navy's LCS shipbuilding contracts require that the ships are built in accordance with the Naval Vessel Rules and other referenced ABS Rules and Guides as necessary to obtain classification. In the absence of ABS, the Navy intends to internally certify those aspects of the LCS designs that were not previously approved by the class society or were subsequently changed.

under high stress and could be prone to failure. Program officials indicated they operated the ship with knowledge of the high-stress areas as a means to field test the strength of the ship. During the initial operating period of LCS 1, cracks emerged in a number of the predicted locations, requiring repair and additional strengthening of LCS 1 and structural modifications during construction of LCS 3.

NAVSEA engineering and SUPSHIP officials indicated that the Navy's decision to cease its arrangement with ABS was also attributed to the view that the class society's role largely duplicated the work being performed by SUPSHIP and Navy engineers. These officials were confident that SUPSHIP was appropriately positioned in terms of the needed skills and resources, as their inspectors were already tasked with overseeing the builders' work to ensure compliance with the specifications. In addition, the officials informed us that NAVSEA's engineering directorate is in the process of revising the Naval Vessel Rules to take into consideration the departure of ABS from the surface combatant shipbuilding programs. SUPSHIP officials told us that a key difference between SUPSHIP's and ABS's inspection processes is the level of discretion the inspectors and surveyors have in determining whether or not work is in accordance with the prescribed rules. Specifically, it is common in commercial shipbuilding for the classification rule set to stipulate that certain work be performed to the satisfaction of the attending surveyor, which gives the classification society surveyors the flexibility to use their professional judgment as to whether or not completed work meets the intent of the rules and is fit for its purpose.[30] According to SUPSHIP officials, the Navy's revised rules will remove such language so that work performed either meets, or does not meet, the applicable technical specifications.

The Navy plans to continue work with ABS in several areas:

- NAVSEA engineering officials informed us that they will continue to contract with ABS on an as-needed basis for design and technical assistance services on new construction surface combatants as a way

---

[30]Specifically, according to officials, the use of the phrase "to the satisfaction of the attending surveyor" in the applicable shipbuilding rule sets is meant to allow the marine surveyor the flexibility to use professional judgment as to whether or not a completed work item is structurally and mechanically suitable for the intended use and application. An item is "fit for service" if it can adequately operate as intended in its as-built condition.

to augment the Navy's skill sets in specialized areas such as structural drawing reviews.

- ABS will continue to provide classification services and issue class certifications to new construction Navy ships operated by the Military Sealift Command.
- Beginning in 2008, Naval Sea Systems Command's Surface Warfare directorate contracted with ABS to perform baseline structural assessments of the condition of the surface combatant fleet when ships are dry-docked for scheduled maintenance after several years of operations.[31] Under this arrangement, scheduled to continue through fiscal year 2016, ABS is conducting marine inspections on 148 surface ships. Using the information obtained during these inspections, ABS is developing models which identify areas of ships where there is an increased risk of failure or corrosion, which allows the Navy the ability to selectively target its maintenance activities.

More recently, in January 2013, the Navy issued a request for information and is seeking input from industry to look into the feasibility of applying commercial shipbuilding design and construction practices on its future amphibious ships. Specifically, the Navy is seeking input from industry regarding the feasibility of building an amphibious ship to ABS's commercial standards while still retaining warship capabilities. One approach identified in the request notification is to use commercial shipbuilding practices for as much of the ship as possible and apply military standards only where necessary.

Conclusions

The Navy pays hundreds of millions and in many cases billions of dollars for ships that warfighters rely on to perform as expected under stressing conditions. Yet it routinely accepts ships with numerous uncorrected deficiencies. Addressing these deficiencies after delivery can be costly, time consuming, and disruptive.

In recent years, Navy leadership has increased its focus on reducing what it considers to be the most serious deficiencies ("starred" deficiencies") at the time of ship delivery with some notable successes. However, the continued practice of accepting ships with a substantial number of deficiencies differs from the commercial practices we observed and can

---

[31]The Achieving Service Life Program is a cooperative agreement established in 2008 between ABS and NAVSEA. The program covers roughly 15-20 ships per year, focusing on those ships with dry-docking availabilities.

be attributed to differing interpretations of what Navy policy requires. Navy policy officials focus on provisions addressing delivery of the ship to the Navy, while program officials focus on the provisions addressing the much later point at which full financial responsibility for the ship is transferred to the operating fleet. This suggests that clarification and consistency in practice is needed. While it is understandable that there may be instances where the Navy would accept delivery of a ship with some level of uncorrected deficiencies, such actions should be the exception rather than the practice. Further, waiting until after delivery to correct known deficiencies can interfere with the activities that should be taking place during this time—ship outfitting, crew training, additional testing, and planned maintenance, as well as other class-wide upgrades. This approach is a sharp contrast to that of commercial ship buyers, who consider quality to be the focus and expect a ship that is defect-free (or nearly so) at delivery.

Navy shipbuilding entails building some of the world's most technologically advanced ships in a limited competitive environment with an industrial base that is generally reliant on the Navy to remain in business—a landscape that is much different than commercial shipbuilding. As such, any quality improvement effort must focus not only on the realities of operating in such an environment, but also on ways to incentivize the shipbuilder to produce a quality product. The Navy's Back to Basics quality improvement effort was directed at SUPSHIP and resulted—albeit in conjunction with other factors—in several positive actions that had an influence on improving quality. While the recent deliveries of the first Joint High Speed Vessel and Mobile Landing Platform represent marked improvements over previous lead ships, continued emphasis on quality and maintaining the momentum created by the Back to Basics initiative is warranted, given that other recently delivered ships had numerous deficiencies.

While the Navy and leading commercial buyers agree that quality is the responsibility of the shipbuilder, a key difference is that the Navy makes use of cost-reimbursement and fixed-price-incentive type contracts, which assign less cost risk to the shipbuilder for quality problems. Leading commercial ship buyers have made a business decision that the risks to quality belong with the shipbuilder, and that the premium paid to transfer this risk is worth the cost of a firm-fixed-price contract. They also make greater use of how payments are structured in the shipbuilding contract to incentivize the builders to ensure timely correction of deficiencies. Even under fixed-price-incentive type contracts, when appropriate, the Navy could choose to structure certain payment provisions to incentivize shipbuilder performance and to enhance contract requirements for managing quality. For example, a standardized quality performance standard, proposed by SUPSHIP, has not been incorporated in any shipbuilding contract.

Commercial shipbuilders also attach considerable importance to having a robust oversight process. A few SUPSHIP locations have begun to make use of some oversight practices emphasized by commercial ship buyers, such as using design drawings, and these practices may be applicable to other locations as well. Further, although SUPSHIP quality inspectors conduct some level of random inspections, the Navy has not defined the role these inspections should play; and we found significant variation in their use among SUPSHIP locations.

Commercial ship buyers also place responsibility for delivering a quality ship on the site team. Responsibility for quality is more diffused in the Navy. Program offices, NAVSEA, SUPSHIP, INSURV, and others all have roles, and concerns about schedule, costs, or other strategic needs may supersede the focus on quality. While SUPSHIP's quality assurance department is closest to the work being performed, the organization has limited authority to make or exert influence on the shipbuilder and on decisions made early in the contracting process that could have a direct impact on quality. The Navy is formulating plans to establish a quality team within the NAVSEA Logistics, Maintenance and Industrial Operations Directorate that would promote, in some capacity, attention to quality assurance, but the roles, responsibilities, and authorities of the team are not yet defined. If the team is given sufficient authorities and tasked with elevating SUPSHIP quality assurance concerns throughout the acquisition process, this could present an opportunity to address some of the issues we identified in our report and emphasize the importance of quality when trade-off decisions affecting cost, schedule, and quality are at hand.

Recommendations for Executive Action

To improve the construction quality of ships delivered to the Navy, we recommend that the Secretary of the Defense direct the Secretary of the Navy to take the following five actions:

1. Ensure that, when established, the NAVSEA-level quality team provides support and a direct link to directors of SUPSHIP quality assurance departments and is tasked with raising concerns within NAVSEA about issues affecting or potentially affecting quality throughout the acquisition process.

2. Clarify Navy policy (Navy Instruction 4700.8J) by clearly identifying at what point(s) during the acquisition process contractor-responsible deficiencies are to be fully corrected and ensure the policy is followed.

3. Provide additional guidance on the quality requirements in shipbuilding contracts, including the extent to which the SUPSHIP Management Group's Quality Performance Standard for Construction of Naval Vessels should be incorporated.

4. Provide additional guidance on use of payment withholds and retentions as a means to incentivize the shipbuilding contractor to promptly correct significant or persistent deficiencies and to deliver a defect-free, or nearly defect free ship, to the Navy.

5. Assess the benefits and determine whether the following practices, in effect at some SUPSHIP locations, would be useful in detecting quality problems across all locations:

   - use of design drawings during SUPSHIP quality inspections, and
   - increased focus on random and in-process inspections compared to use of resources for other types of inspections and observations.

Agency Comments and Our Evaluation

We provided a draft of this report to DOD for comment. In its response, DOD concurred with two of our recommendations and partially concurred with three. DOD's written comments are reproduced in appendix X.

DOD concurred with our first recommendation, and said that it is formulating plans to develop a quality team within the Logistics, Maintenance and Industrial Operations Directorate (NAVSEA 04). This team is envisioned to provide a direct link to SUPSHIP quality assurance departments at the shipyards to enhance communication within NAVSEA on quality related issues. The quality team would also serve as a resource for identifying appropriate quality requirements in shipbuilding contracts.

DOD partially concurred with our second recommendation, to clarify Navy policy regarding acceptance of ships with quality defects. DOD said that it will continue to strive to reduce the number of open deficiencies to zero at the time the ship is delivered to the Navy. The Navy will monitor whether the trend of fewer deficiencies continues to determine if future revisions to the Navy policy instruction are needed. However, we believe the policy needs to be clarified, given the lack of consensus about whether contractor-responsible deficiencies are to be corrected before ships are delivered to the Navy. As we note in the report, addressing deficiencies post-delivery undermines the goal of constructing a defect-free or nearly defect-free ship and can also interfere with testing and crew training. Further, although trends have improved over time, recently delivered ships still had a significant number of deficiencies.

DOD partially concurred with our third recommendation, to provide guidance on quality requirements in contracts. The response cited existing FAR requirements and NAVSEA's Contract Administration Quality Assurance Program. It also stated the planned quality team within NAVSEA 04 will be a resource for consultation on appropriate contract quality assurance provisions and that this, along with the progress in reducing deficiencies, is sufficient. We believe that greater attention to contractual quality provisions is needed. SUPSHIP quality assurance staff stated that a primary reason for the development of the Quality Performance Standard for Construction of Naval Vessels was to limit inconsistencies found in shipbuilding contract quality requirements that affected SUPSHIP's ability to conduct effective quality oversight. As discussed in the report, we observed considerable variance in the specificity of contract quality provisions for different ship classes, and SUPSHIP's suggested quality performance standard has not been fully incorporated in any shipbuilding contract. Therefore we continue to believe that additional guidance on quality, including the extent to which the quality performance standard should be incorporated, would be beneficial for the Navy.

DOD concurred with our fourth recommendation, noting that, as part of its ongoing Better Buying Power initiative, it plans to better align contractor profitability with DOD goals through the use of contract incentives; actions that will assist in improving quality in shipbuilding. DOD explained that as part of this effort, the Office of the Secretary of Defense will revise and reissue guidance on the use of incentives in defense acquisition strategies. Its response noted that new tools, along with existing tools, provide sufficient opportunity for program managers and contracting officers to ensure the construction of quality ships for the Navy.

DOD also partially concurred with our fifth recommendation, to determine whether using design drawings in SUPSHIP quality inspections and increasing the focus on random and in-process inspections would be beneficial. DOD stated that use of design drawings is essential and is being used, but not necessarily by the same personnel that use checklists and other tools for inspections. It also said that random and in-process inspections are all necessary, but that the correct balance should be left to individual ship programs. We found that SUPSHIP quality assurance teams that have trained their staff to use design drawings—a commercial best practice—report benefits from this approach. Also, our work on commercial buyers' quality assurance practices consistently identified random, in-process oversight as a key tool in assuring that shipyards are following their own construction quality processes. DOD's response did not identify any additional actions the Navy plans to take to address our recommendation. We continue to believe that a SUPSHIP-wide assessment of the potential benefits of these practices could yield quality improvements.

DOD also provided technical comments that were incorporated as appropriate. These comments included questions about the deficiency data we reported for the T-AKE ship class. We reviewed individual deficiency reports (trial cards) and compared results with program office and shipbuilder reported data. We resolved anomalies and updated the data on T-AKE presented in this report.

We also provided the Navy shipbuilding contractors, commercial ship buyers, international shipbuilders, and classification societies we met with relevant excerpts of the report and incorporated their technical comments as appropriate.

We are sending copies of this report to the Secretary of Defense, Secretary of the Navy, interested congressional committees, and other interested parties. This report will also be available at no charge on GAO's website at http://www.gao.gov.

If you or your staff have any questions concerning this report, please contact me at (202) 512-4841 or by e-mail at mackinm@gao.gov. Contact points for our Offices of Congressional Relations and Public Affairs may be found on the last page of this report. Key contributors to this report are listed in appendix XI.

Michele Mackin

Michele Mackin, Director
Acquisition and Sourcing Management

List of Committees

The Honorable Carl Levin
Chairman
The Honorable James M. Inhofe
Ranking Member
Committee on Armed Services
United States Senate

The Honorable Howard P. "Buck" McKeon
Chairman
The Honorable Adam Smith
Ranking Member
Committee on Armed Services
House of Representatives

The Honorable Richard J. Durbin
Chairman
The Honorable Thad Cochran
Ranking Member
Subcommittee on Defense
Committee on Appropriations
United States Senate

The Honorable Rodney Frelinghuysen
Chairman
The Honorable Pete Visclosky
Ranking Member
Subcommittee on Defense
Committee on Appropriations
House of Representatives

Appendix I: Objectives, Scope, and Methodology

To identify the extent to which newly constructed Navy ships had quality problems and the actions that Navy has taken to improve quality, we reviewed the Navy's Board of Inspection and Survey reports for all Navy ships delivered from 2006 through May 2013: including *Arleigh Burke* class (DDG 51) destroyers, USS *George H. W. Bush* (CVN 77) aircraft carrier, USNS *Howard O. Lorenzen* (T-AGM 25) missile range instrumentation ship, *Lewis and Clark*-class (T-AKE) dry cargo and ammunition ships, Littoral Combat Ship (LCS)—both the *Independence and Freedom* variants, USS *Makin Island* (LHD 8) Wasp-class amphibious assault ship, USNS *Montford Point* Mobile Landing Platform, *San Antonio*-class (LPD 17) amphibious transport dock ships, USNS *Spearhead* Joint High Speed Vessel, and *Virginia*-class submarines (SSN 774). Even though the lead LPD and SSN ships were built outside of the last 8 years, we included these two vessels in our sample because the rest of the class was built within the last 8 years. We also drew from our prior work on these programs, Navy documents created to address quality issues, and various other Navy reports, such as those from the Navy's Judge Advocate General.

To determine the number and type of deficiencies for each vessel, we obtained data from the Navy's Board of Inspection and Survey's (INSURV) Material Inspection data warehouse and the Navy's Technical Support Management (TSM) system. TSM is the primary database the Navy's Supervisor of Shipbuilding, Conversion and Repair uses to track the status of new ship construction deficiencies. We analyzed these data to determine the total number of open deficiencies (1) when the ship was delivered to the Navy; (2) 120 days following ship delivery—the approximate time when final outfitting is completed prior to the ship leaving the shipyard; and (3) 1 year following ship delivery. Total deficiencies include those identified during construction, builder's trials, and acceptance trials that were not closed by the milestones listed above. Because TSM deficiency data is compiled on paper forms and manually entered into the system, we considered as being closed at delivery those deficiencies that were closed through 7 days following the date the ship was delivered to the Navy (with the exception of the T-AKE ship class), as stated on the Navy's Naval Vessel Register. To the extent feasible, we reviewed these data for completeness and for obvious inconsistency errors and compared them with paper documents that also catalogue these deficiencies. When we found obvious discrepancies while conducting our analyses, we brought them to the attention of the Navy Sea Systems Command and INSURV and worked with them to understand, correct, or omit the discrepancies. The data we collected represents the deficiencies at a particular moment in time. Further,

deficiencies may be subdivided into multiple deficiencies or consolidated
into a smaller number when the Navy and its shipbuilding contractors
determine whether the government or the shipbuilder is responsible for
correcting the respective deficiencies. For ships we reviewed, we
determined that TSM deficiency data were sufficiently reliable for the
purposes of this report with a few exceptions. These exceptions relate to
data for T-AKE class ships. TSM data did not cover T-AKE 1 through T-
AKE 6. Data for T-AKE 12 had numerous data errors and is therefore not
reported on. For other T-AKE ships, we reviewed deficiency
documentation (trial cards) to resolve discrepancies between TSM and T-
AKE program office data.

We catalogued several hull, mechanical, and electrical issues with each
ship class delivered in the last 8 years, in addition to the individual hulls
that were also delivered during this period. To create this list of illustrative
examples, we asked Navy officials familiar with each ship class to identify
problems that occurred during the construction of the vessels. We also
asked officials from INSURV to identify significant issues that affected
multiple hulls within each major class. We then identified several of the
issues to highlight that were illustrative of hull, mechanical, and electrical
problems. Given the uniqueness of the ships' capabilities, we elected not
to catalog quality issues with weapon systems or other warfighting
systems. To supplement this analysis, we held discussions with or
requested information from a number of Navy officials involved in Navy
shipbuilding. These included the Supervisor of Shipbuilding, Conversion
and Repair (SUPSHIP), Bath, Maine; Groton, Connecticut; Gulf Coast,
Pascagoula, Mississippi; Newport News, Virginia; Bath Detachment, San
Diego, California; Bath Detachment, Marinette, Wisconsin; and Gulf
Coast Detachment, Mobile, Alabama. We also interviewed the Director of
the Board of Inspection and Survey and officials in the Naval Sea
Systems Command Management Group for SUPSHIP; Naval Sea
Systems Command Contracting Directorate; Naval Sea Systems
Command Engineering Directorate; Naval Sea Systems Command
Surface Warfare Directorate; Naval Sea Systems Command Nuclear
Propulsion; Program Executive Offices for Carriers; Program Executive
Office for Submarines, and the Littoral Combat Ship; representatives from
acquisition program offices including PMS 317 (LPD 17), PMS 377 (LHD
8 and LHA 6), PMS 385 (Joint High Speed Vessel and Mobile Landing
Platform), PMS 400 D (DDG 51), and, PMS 501 (LCS); Norfolk Ship
Support Activity—Regional Maintenance Center; Southwest Regional
Maintenance Center; Commander, Operational Test and Evaluation
Force; Military Sealift Command; Fleet Forces Command; and the
Defense Contract Management Agency.

We also visited eight U.S. Navy contractor shipyards that build some of
the larger Navy vessels and met with representatives from the contractor
that owns each shipyard, including Austal USA in Mobile, Alabama;
General Dynamics Electric Boat Corporation in Groton, Connecticut and
Quonset Point, Rhode Island; General Dynamics NASSCO in San Diego,
California, and General Dynamics Bath Iron Works in Bath, Maine;
Huntington Ingalls Industries Ingalls Shipbuilding in Pascagoula,
Mississippi and Huntington Ingalls Industries Newport News Shipbuilding
in Newport News, Virginia; Marinette Marine Corporation in Marinette,
Wisconsin; and, V.T. Halter Marine at its shipyard in Pascagoula,
Mississippi. In addition, we observed the underway portion of the
acceptance trial for T-AKE 13 in San Diego, California.

Lastly, we reviewed the Navy's efforts to improve ship quality by
reviewing key memos and documents outlining the Back to Basics
program and meeting with the officials responsible for implementing these
efforts—most of whom were in the Navy's Supervisor of Shipbuilding,
Conversion and Repair commands. We also reviewed selected parts of
11 fixed-priced-incentive and firm-fixed priced Navy shipbuilding
contracts, such as clauses pertaining to quality requirements and ship
delivery, for *San Antonio* class (LPD 17) amphibious transport dock ships
(one contract); *America* class (LHA 6 and LHA 7) amphibious assault ship
(two contracts); *Arleigh Burke* class (DDG 51) destroyer (one contract);
Joint High Speed Vessel (one contract); Littoral Combat Ship (LCS)—
Freedom and *Independence* variants (two contracts); *Lewis and Clark*
class (T-AKE) dry cargo and ammunition ship (one contract); USNS
Howard O. Lorenzen (T-AGM 25) missile instrumentation ship (one
contract) ; USS *Makin Island* (LHD 8) amphibious assault ship (one
contract); and the Mobile Landing Platform (one contract).

To assess key practices used by commercial ship buyers and
shipbuilders, we interviewed and met with leading commercial companies
from the cruise, oil and gas, and commercial shipping industries, including
Carnival Corporation; Chevron Corporation; Ensco plc; ExxonMobil; A.P.
Moller-Maersk A/S; Noble Corporation; Norwegian Cruise Lines; Royal
Caribbean Cruises, Ltd.; and Seadrill, Ltd. We identified leading
companies by analyzing such indicators as annual sales, number of
vessels owned and procured, and total market share. Our methodology
drew from our previous shipbuilding best practices work that identified the
commercial shipbuilding industries that support cruise, oil and gas, and
commercial shipping sectors as being most similar to Navy shipbuilding.
Cruise ships are more costly and complex than other types of commercial
ships, densely packed, and require significant outfitting, making them

somewhat similar to military ships. Additionally, cruise ship buyers often
include innovations or design changes in their ships and start new
classes of ships regularly in order to maximize passenger satisfaction;
approaches that allowed us to examine quality oversight practices on
recent lead ship programs and the outcomes of specific commercial
practices. The cruise line companies we met with are leaders in their
industry as identified in our previous work and based on operating
revenue or fleet size. We met with ship buyers from the oil and gas
industry because drill ships, floating production storage and offloading
(FPSO) vessels and offshore oil platforms are complex, dense structures.
Furthermore, FPSOs, essentially floating refineries, are often one of a
kind, costing well over $1 billion. The oil and gas companies we met with
are leaders in their industry as identified in our previous work as well as
our assessment of top operators of drilling vessels. Similarly, we met with
Maersk Line Limited and Maersk Drilling, two business units within A.P.
Moller-Maersk A/S, because the company was identified as an industry
leader in our prior work and remains one of the largest shipping
companies in the world. For example, Maersk Line Limited acquires many
ships: in 2012 the company took delivery of 19 new ships. For each
commercial ship buyer, we requested deficiency data on one or more new
construction ships they had acquired. With the exception of one FPSO, all
of these ships were delivered to the buyer in 2012 or 2013. We assessed
the reliability of this data by obtaining information on the systems that
stored the data and interviewing ship buyer and shipbuilder
representatives knowledgeable about the data. We determined that the
data were sufficiently reliable for the purposes of this report. We also
identified common processes and tools used by these ship buyers and
shipbuilders to ensure the expected level of quality.

To determine the extent to which Navy quality assurance processes use
common commercial practices, we reviewed data and information
obtained from the Navy and its shipbuilding contractors, as well as from
the leading commercial ship buyers and shipbuilders. We also reviewed
relevant payment and retention clauses for 11 fixed-priced Navy
shipbuilding contracts. During our meetings with SUPSHIP and program,
engineering, and contracting officials from the Naval Sea Systems
Command directorates, we inquired about the Navy's quality assurance
practices. During site visits to eight U.S. private shipyards that build Navy
ships, we discussed with shipyard representatives their quality assurance
processes and the steps taken to ensure their ships meet the Navy's
quality expectations. During our site visits, we collected documentation
related to the shipyard's quality assurance activities, including quality

policies, plans, and procedures, and we also observed quality assurance
inspection activities when possible.

We also met with officials from international commercial shipyards that
are responsible for building a variety of complex ships, including Meyer
Werft (Germany) and STX Finland (Finland), which both build cruise
ships; and Hyundai Heavy Industries and Daewoo Shipbuilding and
Marine Engineering (South Korea), which build commercial ships,
including containerships, liquefied natural gas carriers, drill ships, FPSOs,
and oil tankers. We identified these shipbuilders as producers of high-
quality vessels through a combination of our previous work and
recommendations from shipbuilding experts and the ship buyers that
participated in our review. At the shipyards, we met with ship buyers'
representatives who were responsible for overseeing the construction of
the ships and monitoring the construction schedule. Where possible, we
observed quality assurance activities at commercial shipbuilders or
viewed systems related to ensuring quality, such as quality database
systems. We collected documentation of quality assurance activities,
such as quality policies and inspection plans, where available. We met
with representatives from three classification societies, including the
American Bureau of Shipping (ABS), Det Norske Veritas, and Lloyd's
Register regarding their roles in commercial ship construction. We also
met with representatives from Aker Shipyard in Philadelphia,
Pennsylvania, to discuss how a U.S. shipbuilder that solely builds
commercial vessels approaches quality assurance.

To better understand the role of classification societies in Navy and
commercial shipbuilding, we met with engineering and marine surveying
representatives from ABS to obtain an overview of how they conduct their
work. We held discussions on the role of classification in Navy
shipbuilding with Navy shipbuilding contractors, including Austal USA,
Mobile, Alabama; General Dynamics Bath Iron Works, Bath, Maine;
General Dynamics NASSCO, San Diego, California; Marinette Marine
Corporation, Marinette, Wisconsin; and V.T. Halter Marine, Pascagoula,
Mississippi. To learn the extent to which the Navy's approach to new ship
construction oversight is similar to or different than the marine surveying
services provided by ABS during construction of Navy ships, we met with
officials from SUPSHIP locations at Bath, Maine; Bath Detachment, San
Diego, California; Bath Detachment, Marinette, Wisconsin; Gulf Coast,
Pascagoula, Mississippi; and Mobile, Alabama. We also held discussions
on this matter with officials from the Naval Sea Systems Command
SUPSHIP Management Group; Military Sealift Command; Naval Sea
Systems Command Engineering Directorate; Naval Sea Systems

Command Surface Warfare Directorate; Program Executive Office Littoral Combat Ship; and representatives from acquisition program offices including PMS 385 (Joint High Speed Vessel and Mobile Landing Platform). We reviewed the classification rule set developed by the Navy and ABS (the Naval Vessel Rules), as well as other classification rule sets pertaining to Navy and or commercial vessels, such as High-Speed Naval Craft rules and the Steel Vessel rules. In addition, we reviewed the findings and observations of ABS's marine surveyors for the Littoral Combat Ship which is being built in accordance with the Naval Vessel Rules, as well as the Joint High Speed Vessel, which is built in accordance with ABS's Naval High Speed Naval Craft Guide. We also spoke with representatives from other classification societies, including Det Norske Veritas and Lloyd's Register, to discuss their approach to classification of commercial and navy vessels. When meeting with commercial ship buyers and shipbuilders, we also discussed the ship classification process and the role of classification societies in shipbuilding.

We conducted this performance audit from March 2012 to November 2013 in accordance with generally accepted government auditing standards. Those standards require that we plan and perform the audit to obtain sufficient, appropriate evidence to provide a reasonable basis for our findings and conclusions based on our audit objectives. We believe that the evidence obtained provides a reasonable basis for our findings and conclusions based on our audit objectives.

Appendix II: Stages of Shipbuilding

There are four primary phases in shipbuilding: pre-contracting, contract award, design and planning, and construction, with each phase building upon the work completed in earlier stages. Within each phase, a number of key events have an influence on the overall quality of the ship. In addition, within Navy shipbuilding, additional key activities take place following ship delivery. Table 2 describes some of the more significant events occurring throughout the shipbuilding process.

Table 2: Key Events Occurring During Navy and Commercial Shipbuilding

Stage	Key event	Description
Pre-contracting activities Contract award	Concept refinement	Ship buyer determines necessary requirements and desired capabilities, develops an acquisition strategy.
	Early-stage design	Ship buyer refines its operational and performance requirements into specifications that will be included in the shipbuilding contract.
	Contract award and negotiation	Ship buyer selects and enters into a shipbuilding contract with the chosen shipbuilder(s). The contract includes the ship's specification, which details how the shipbuilder will build the ship and meet the buyer's requirements.
Design and planning	Detailed engineering design	Ship designer develops all aspects of the ship's structure and routing of major distributive systems, such as electrical or piping, throughout the ship. A three-dimension (3D) computer-aided-design model is often generated, along with completion of any computer modeling or simulation analyses, such as those to test the structural integrity of the ship design throughout its service life or under certain sea conditions.
	Pre-construction and planning activities	Shipbuilder plans production flow and develops two-dimensional paper drawings that, once approved by the ship buyer, will be used by shipyard workers to build the ship. Ship buyer, shipbuilder, and classification society (if applicable) collectively determine quality-related test and inspection points during ship construction.
Construction	Steel cutting/block fabrication	Ship fabrication begins as large steel or aluminum plates are cut and welded to form the basic building units for a ship called "blocks." Blocks comprise compartments, which include accommodation space, engine room, and storage areas.
	Assembly and outfitting of blocks	Upon completion of a block, piping, brackets for machinery or cabling, and ladders, among other things, are installed. Installing these items at this stage is preferable because access to spaces is not limited by doors or other machinery, requiring less time and effort than at later stages of construction.
	Keel laying and block erection	Blocks are welded to form larger sections, referred to as grand blocks, which comprise the ship's structure. The shipbuilder then assembles and welds grand blocks and blocks in the drydock to form the keel. Machinery, engines, propeller shafts and other large items are also installed during this stage.
	Launch	Once the ship is watertight, the drydock is flooded and the ship is towed to a docking area where final outfitting of machinery and equipment occur.[a]

Stage	Key event	Description
	System testing and commissioning	Parts, materials, and machinery, such as engines, pumps, and associated control instrumentation used in the ship, are generally tested by the manufacturer (factory acceptance test) to ensure quality standards, technical specifications, and performance requirements are met. Installation and connection of these components create subsystems. The shipbuilder and ship buyer ensure the subsystems and systems are installed in accordance to the ship's specifications and conduct tests to ensure systems are operating as intended and meet performance requirements.
	Sea trials	Once the shipbuilder is satisfied that the ship is seaworthy and meets the buyer's requirements, the ship buyer's representatives, and if applicable the classification society's surveyors, are brought onboard and the ship embarks on a series of dockside and at-sea tests where the overall quality and performance of the ship is evaluated against the contractually required specifications. Sea trials provide early verification of the buyer's requirements and allow time for any corrective actions that may be required to meet the buyer's requirements prior to ship delivery. Navy shipbuilding programs generally conduct two sets of sea trials—builder's trials and acceptance trials. Builder's trials test the vessel's propulsion, communications, navigation and mission systems, as well as all related support systems. Following the successful completion of builder's trials, acceptance trials are conducted by the Navy's Board of Inspection and Survey (INSURV).
	Delivery/Acceptance	Ship buyer takes custody and assumes ownership of the vessel. In the commercial world, the ship is complete and commences operations. In Navy shipbuilding, a Material Inspection and Receiving Report (Form DD 250) is prepared, representing the official transfer of custody and ownership to the Navy. Any unresolved deficiencies or remaining work items are segregated by the entity that is responsible for completion of the work (Navy or shipbuilder) and identified on this document.
Post-delivery activities specific to the Navy	Final outfitting	Crew boards the ship and begins training; and mission systems are installed.[b]
	Post-delivery tests and trials	Operational tests are conducted on the ships combat and mission critical systems.
	Final contract trials	INSURV conducts a second round of sea trials just prior to the expiration of the ship's guarantee period.[c]
	Post Shakedown Availability	Planned maintenance period prior to the maiden voyage where work is performed to install class-wide upgrades or ship improvements, perform maintenance, and correct new or previously identified construction deficiencies. Usually performed using a different contract than shipbuilding contract.
	Shipbuilding and Conversion, Navy Obligation and Work Limiting Date	The official date where full responsibility for funding the ship's operation and maintenance is transferred from the acquisition command to the operational fleet.

Source: GAO analysis of Navy and industry provided data.

[a]The level of outfitting completed prior to launch varies by shipbuilder and ship type, but is predetermined according to the builder's production plan. Shipbuilders generally agree that launching a ship having a lower level of outfitting completed than what was planned can increase the costs to complete the work.

[b]On nuclear-powered Navy ships, the ship's crew begins boarding and training prior to ship delivery.

[c]The guarantee period is the time after delivery where the shipbuilder is responsible for correcting any defects or deficiencies in accordance to the terms and conditions of the contract.

Appendix III: *Lewis and Clark* Dry Cargo and Ammunition Ship Class (T-AKE)

The *Lewis and Clark* class of dry cargo and ammunition ships (T-AKE 1) consists of 14 ships which have been delivered to the Navy. The first ship was delivered in 2006 and the final ship was delivered in 2012.

We analyzed data provided by the Supervisor of Shipbuilding, Conversion, and Repair (SUPSHIP) to determine the number of open deficiencies at delivery, 120 days after delivery, and one year after delivery. Our analysis of the available data found that recently delivered T-AKEs had noticeably fewer open deficiencies at delivery compared to other ship classes. Unlike other classes in our review, the Navy was responsible for the majority of these deficiencies.

Table 3: Open Deficiencies on T-AKE Class Ships at Various Points in Time after Delivery

Ship (delivery date)	Importance[b]	Delivery[a]		120 days after delivery		365 days after delivery	
		Total deficiencies[c]	Percentage of contractor-responsible deficiencies[d]	Total deficiencies	Percentage of contractor-responsible deficiencies	Total deficiencies	Percentage of contractor-responsible deficiencies
T-AKE 7 (March 2009)	Part 1	22	5	5	0	1	0
	Part 2	154	1	44	2	3	0
	Part 3	3	0	2	0	0	0
T-AKE 8 (September 2009)	Part 1	5	20	0	0	0	0
	Part 2	40	18	18	6	2	50
	Part 3	1	0	0	33	0	0
T-AKE 9 (February 2010)	Part 1	29	8	4	25	1	100
	Part 2	136	2	14	7	1	100
	Part 3	5	0	0	0	0	0
T-AKE 10 (July 2010)	Part 1	5	40	5	40	4	50
	Part 2	39	8	21	14	10	10
	Part 3	0	0	0	0	0	0
T-AKE 11 (February 2011)	Part 1	6	0	1	0	0	0
	Part 2	17	12	5	20	2	50
	Part 3	0	0	0	0	0	0
T-AKE 13 (April 2012)	Part 1	3	0	2	0	1	0
	Part 2	32	4	24	4	4	0
	Part 3	0	0	0	0	0	0
T-AKE 14	Part 1	3	0	0	0	-	-

Ship (delivery date)	Importance[b]	Delivery[a]		120 days after delivery		365 days after delivery	
		Total deficiencies[c]	Percentage of contractor-responsible deficiencies[d]	Total deficiencies	Percentage of contractor-responsible deficiencies	Total deficiencies	Percentage of contractor-responsible deficiencies
(October 2012)	Part 2	21	0	1	0	-	-
	Part 3	0	0	0	0	-	-

Source: GAO analysis of Navy data as of March 2013.

Notes: (1) TSM relies on user-entered information, which can be unreliable. T-AKE 12's TSM data did not pass our data reliability standards because 98 percent of the deficiencies were opened and closed in the system on the same day—a date after the ship had been delivered to the Navy. (2) Deficiencies with missing Importance designations are not included in this table.

[a]The table counts deficiencies from the Navy's Technical Support Management (TSM) system which were closed after the official delivery date listed in the Naval Vessel Register, www.nvr.navy.mil, including those deficiencies where it was subsequently determined no further corrective action would be taken. In some instances, similar types of deficiencies were consolidated into a single deficiency prior to ship delivery. In other instances, uncorrected deficiencies were closed and transferred to final contract trials deficiencies (trial cards).

[b]Deficiencies are numbered by their significance and order of importance as Part 1, Part 2, and Part 3. The Navy's Board of Inspection and Survey (INSURV) defines a Part 1 deficiency is an important deficiency which is likely to cause the ship to be unseaworthy, substantially reduce the ability of the ship to carry out an assigned mission, or cause serious injury to personnel or serious damage to important material or equipment. According to INSURV, Part 2 deficiencies are less significant or do not meet the criteria for Part 1 deficiencies, but should be corrected to restore the ship to required specifications. INSURV classifies Part 3 deficiencies as those that will require either major alterations to correct (design related) or modifications that are too costly to effect during the life cycle of the ship.

[c]The Navy's Board of Inspection and Survey (INSURV) documents all deficiencies which require corrective action to bring the material condition of the ship to required specifications. Deficiencies may have been identified during INSURV or builder's trials.

[d]Percentage is rounded to the nearest whole percent. Navy program managers and SUPSHIP may assign responsibility for correcting a deficiency to the contractor if the contractor, sub-contractors, or vendors do not meet the requirements of the shipbuilding contract. Where data were available, we determined the percent of Part 1, Part 2, Part 3, and total deficiencies designated as contractor-responsible versus government-responsible. In some cases, the responsible party for correcting a deficiency may alternate between the Navy and the contractor based on additional investigations into the issues.

Appendix IV: *San Antonio* Amphibious Transport Dock Ship Class (LPD 17)

The *San Antonio* class of amphibious transport docks (LPD 17) consists of eight ships which have been delivered to the Navy. The first ship was delivered in 2005. As of September 2013, the Navy has three ships under construction. The *San Antonio* class has generally seen a decline in the number of open deficiencies at delivery, yet each ship still has a large number of open deficiencies.

We analyzed data provided by the Supervisor of Shipbuilding, Conversion, and Repair (SUPSHIP) to determine the number of open deficiencies at delivery, 120 days after delivery, and one year after delivery. Our analysis found that recently delivered ships had thousands of open deficiencies, ranging from 1,403 on LPD 23 to 6,325 on LPD 21. The majority of the deficiencies open at delivery were the responsibility of the contractor with the exception of LPD 23 where only 40 percent of the open deficiencies were the contractor's responsibility. The data below indicates that many of these deficiencies are being closed after the ships are delivered to the Navy and are being outfitted.

Table 4: Open Deficiencies on LPD 17 Class Ships at Various Points in Time after Delivery

Ship (delivery date)	Importance[b]	Delivery[a]		120 days after delivery		365 days after delivery	
		Total deficiencies[c]	Percentage of contractor-responsible deficiencies[d]	Total deficiencies	Percentage of contractor-responsible deficiencies	Total deficiencies	Percentage of contractor-responsible deficiencies
LPD 21 (August 2009)	Part 1	234	58	75	28	23	26
	Part 2	6,078	79	1,385	49	465	57
	Part 3	13	23	0	0	0	0
LPD 22 (December 2011)	Part 1	156	25	102	5	47	2
	Part 2	4,783	69	1,074	49	453	57
	Part 3	24	63	1	100	0	0
LPD 23 (September 2012)	Part 1	88	25	55	18	-	-
	Part 2	1,270	42	685	51	-	-
	Part 3	45	2	37	0	-	-
LPD 24 (December 2012)	Part 1	86	48	36	25	-	-
	Part 2	1,891	58	667	48	-	-
	Part 3	28	25	15	13	-	-

Source: GAO analysis of Navy data as of March 2013.

Notes: (1) Deficiencies with missing Importance designations are not included in this table.

[a]For the purposes of this report, the table counts deficiencies from the Navy's Technical Support Management (TSM) system which were closed seven days or more after the official delivery date listed in the Naval Vessel Register, www.nvr.navy.mil. Deficiencies closed after delivery but before the seventh day are not included.

[b]Deficiencies are numbered by their significance and order of importance as Part 1, Part 2, and Part 3. INSURV defines a Part 1 deficiency is an important deficiency which is likely to cause the ship to be unseaworthy, substantially reduce the ability of the ship to carry out an assigned mission, or cause serious injury to personnel or serious damage to important material or equipment. According to INSURV, Part 2 deficiencies are less significant or do not meet the criteria for Part 1 deficiencies, but should be corrected to restore the ship to required specifications. INSURV classifies Part 3 deficiencies as those that will require either major alterations to correct (design-related) or modifications that are too costly to effect during the life cycle of the ship.

[c] The Navy's Board of Inspection and Survey (INSURV) documents all deficiencies which require corrective action to bring the material condition of the ship to required specifications. Deficiencies may have been identified during INSURV or builder's trials.

[d]Percentage is rounded to the nearest whole percent. Navy program managers and SUPSHIP may assign responsibility for correcting a deficiency to the contractor if the contractor, sub-contractors, or vendors do not meet the requirements of the shipbuilding contract. Where data were available, we determined the percent of Part 1, Part 2, Part 3, and total deficiencies designated as contractor-responsible versus government-responsible. In some cases, the responsible party for correcting a deficiency may alternate between the Navy and the contractor based on additional investigations into the issues.

Appendix V: Littoral Combat Ship (LCS) Class

The Littoral Combat Ship (LCS) class consists of 3 ships which had been delivered to the Navy at the time of our review. The first hull was delivered in 2008. Currently, the Navy has seven ships under construction and has received funding to construct six ships. The Navy has an additional eight ships under contract which are not yet funded. The LCS class consists of two different seaframe designs, the LCS 1 design (*Freedom* variant) and the LCS 2 design (*Independence* variant).

We analyzed data provided by the Supervisor of Shipbuilding, Conversion, and Repair (SUPSHIP) to determine the number of open deficiencies at delivery, 120 days after delivery, and one year after delivery. Our analysis found that both designs of the LCS class were delivered with a large number of open deficiencies at delivery. The majority of these deficiencies were the responsibility of the contractor. Our analysis found that over half of these deficiencies were closed after the ships were delivered to the Navy and were being outfitted.

Table 5: Open Deficiencies on LCS Class Ships at Various Points in Time after Delivery

Ship (Delivery date)	Importance[b]	Delivery[a]		120 days after delivery		365 days after delivery	
		Total deficiencies[c]	Percentage of contractor-responsible deficiencies[d]	Total deficiencies	Percentage of contractor-responsible deficiencies	Total deficiencies	Percentage of contractor-responsible deficiencies
LCS 1 (September 2008)	Part 1	151	72	86	62	30	37
	Part 2	1,994	81	988	76	175	46
	Part 3	109	82	56	77	11	36
LCS 2 (December 2009)	Part 1	547	81	256	71	131	64
	Part 2	3,715	71	2,079	60	819	56
	Part 3	954	82	510	74	213	62
LCS 3 (June 2012)	Part 1	103	57	40	63	-	-
	Part 2	1,178	75	482	65	-	-
	Part 3	18	50	5	80	-	-

Source: GAO analysis of Navy data as of March 2013.

Notes: (1) Odd numbered LCS class ships (*Freedom* variant) are built at a Navy contractor shipyard in Marinette, Wisconsin, while even numbered ships (*Independence* variant) are built at a Navy contractor shipyard in Mobile, Alabama. (2) Deficiencies with missing Importance designations are not included in this table.

[a]For the purposes of this report, the table counts deficiencies from the Navy's Technical Support Management (TSM) system which were closed seven days or more after the official delivery date listed in the Naval Vessel Register, www.nvr.navy.mil. Deficiencies closed after delivery but before the seventh day are not included.

[b]Deficiencies are numbered by their significance and order of importance as Part 1, Part 2, and Part 3. INSURV defines a Part 1 deficiency is an important deficiency which is likely to cause the ship to be unseaworthy, substantially reduce the ability of the ship to carry out an assigned mission, or cause serious injury to personnel or serious damage to important material or equipment. According to INSURV, Part 2 deficiencies are less significant or do not meet the criteria for Part 1 deficiencies, but should be corrected to restore the ship to required specifications. INSURV classifies Part 3 deficiencies as those that will require either major alterations to correct (design related) or modifications that are too costly to effect during the life cycle of the ship.

[c]The Navy's Board of Inspection and Survey (INSURV) documents all deficiencies which require corrective action to bring the material condition of the ship to required specifications. Deficiencies may have been identified during INSURV or builder's trials.

[d]Percentage is rounded to the nearest whole percent. Navy program managers and SUPSHIP may assign responsibility for correcting a deficiency to the contractor if the contractor, sub-contractors, or vendors do not meet the requirements of the shipbuilding contract. Where data were available, we determined the percent of Part 1, Part 2, Part 3, and total deficiencies designated as contractor-responsible versus government-responsible. In some cases, the responsible party for correcting a deficiency may alternate between the Navy and the contractor based on additional investigations into the issues.

Appendix VI: *Arleigh Burke* Guided Missile Destroyer Ship Class (DDG 51)

The *Arleigh Burke* class of guided missile destroyers (DDG 51) consists of 62 ships which had been delivered to the Navy at the time of our review. The first ship was delivered in 1991. Currently, the Navy has received funding to construct an additional four ships. Despite being a well established program, the *Arleigh Burke* class continues to have a large number of open deficiencies at various points in time.

We analyzed data provided by the Supervisor of Shipbuilding, Conversion, and Repair (SUPSHIP) to determine the number of open deficiencies at delivery, 120 days after delivery, and one year after delivery. Our analysis found that recently delivered ships had a large number of open deficiencies, ranging from a low of 333 open deficiencies on DDG 110 to a high of 4,385 open deficiencies on DDG 109. The majority of the deficiencies open at delivery were the responsibility of the contractor. The data below indicates that many of these deficiencies were being closed after the ships had been delivered to the Navy and were being outfitted.

Table 6: Open Deficiencies on DDG 51 Class Ships at Various Points in Time after Delivery

Ship (delivery date)	Importance[b]	Delivery[a]		120 days after delivery		365 days after delivery	
		Total deficiencies[c]	Percentage of contractor-responsible deficiencies[d]	Total deficiencies	Percentage of contractor-responsible deficiencies	Total deficiencies	Percentage of contractor-responsible deficiencies
DDG 108 (July 2009)	Part 1	38	47	17	0	6	0
	Part 2	1,186	72	100	11	52	4
	Part 3	1,981	90	94	24	23	35
DDG 105 (August 2009)	Part 1	96	70	15	27	8	50
	Part 2	1,453	73	116	33	61	61
	Part 3	487	92	22	59	19	68
DDG 109 (June 2010)	Part 1	52	71	10	20	3	67
	Part 2	2,483	81	172	36	59	8
	Part 3	1,850	90	122	63	29	14
DDG 107 (July 2010)	Part 1	16	56	7	14	4	25
	Part 2	672	63	61	38	31	29
	Part 3	235	86	7	71	3	100
DDG 110 (February 2011)	Part 1	12	25	8	13	4	25
	Part 2	285	59	55	33	36	36
	Part 3	35	66	1	0	0	0
DDG 111	Part 1	17	29	5	0	2	0

Ship (delivery date)	Importance[b]	Delivery[a]		120 days after delivery		365 days after delivery	
		Total deficiencies[c]	Percentage of contractor-responsible deficiencies[d]	Total deficiencies	Percentage of contractor-responsible deficiencies	Total deficiencies	Percentage of contractor-responsible deficiencies
(April 2011)	Part 2	2,057	74	279	36	140	15
	Part 3	1,896	92	152	63	41	5
DDG 112 (May 2012)	Part 1	20	20	5	0	-	-
	Part 2	1,085	55	159	20	-	-
	Part 3	0	0	0	0	-	-

Source: GAO analysis of Navy data as of March 2013.

Notes: (1) DDG 51 class ships are built at two Navy contractor shipyards in Bath, Maine and Pascagoula, Mississippi. (2) The ships are presented in chronological based on the date of delivery to the Navy. (3) Deficiencies with missing Importance designations are not included in this table.

[a]For the purposes of this report, the table counts deficiencies from the Navy's Technical Support Management (TSM) system which were closed seven days or more after the official delivery date listed in the Naval Vessel Register, www.nvr.navy.mil. Deficiencies closed after delivery but before the seventh day are not included.

[b]Deficiencies are numbered by their significance and order of importance as Part 1, Part 2, and Part 3. INSURV defines a Part 1 deficiency is an important deficiency which is likely to cause the ship to be unseaworthy, substantially reduce the ability of the ship to carry out an assigned mission, or cause serious injury to personnel or serious damage to important material or equipment. According to INSURV, Part 2 deficiencies are less significant or do not meet the criteria for Part 1 deficiencies, but should be corrected to restore the ship to required specifications. INSURV classifies Part 3 deficiencies as those that will require either major alterations to correct (design related) or modifications that are too costly to effect during the life cycle of the ship.

[c]The Navy's Board of Inspection and Survey (INSURV) documents all deficiencies which require corrective action to bring the material condition of the ship to required specifications. Deficiencies may have been identified during INSURV or builder's trials.

[d]Percentage is rounded to the nearest whole percent. Navy program managers and SUPSHIP may assign responsibility for correcting a deficiency to the contractor if the contractor, sub-contractors, or vendors do not meet the requirements of the shipbuilding contract. Where data were available, we determined the percent of Part 1, Part 2, Part 3, and total deficiencies designated as contractor-responsible versus government-responsible. In some cases, the responsible party for correcting a deficiency may alternate between the Navy and the contractor based on additional investigations into the issues.

Figure 16: Selected Quality Issues on *USS George H.W. Bush* (CVN 77)

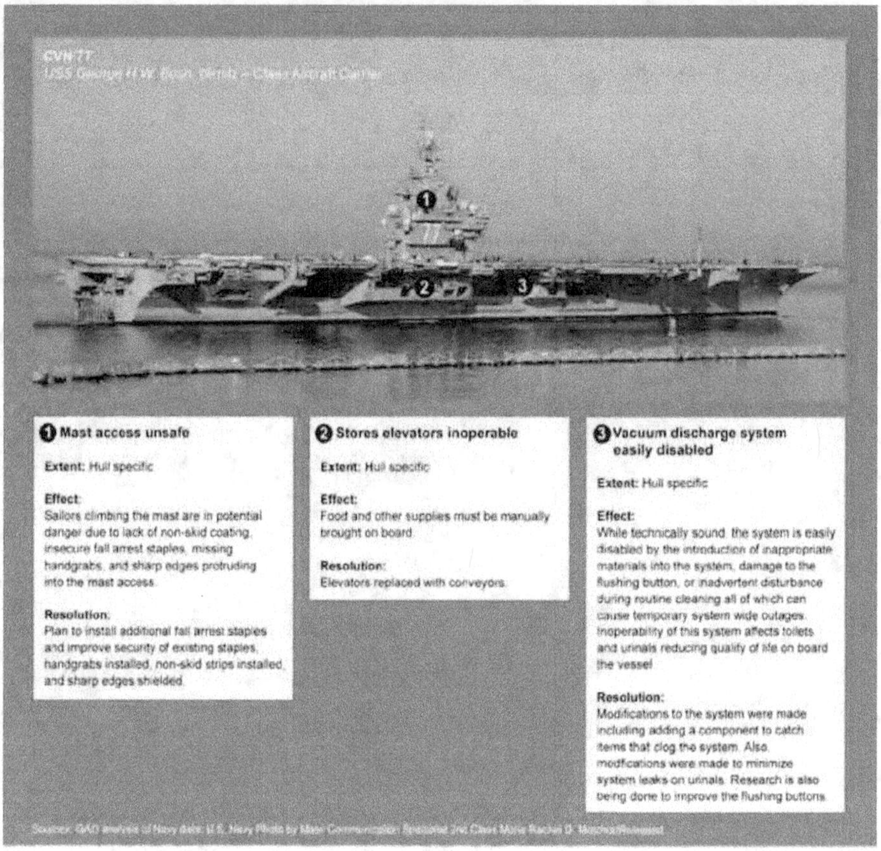

CVN 77
USS George H.W. Bush, Nimitz – Class Aircraft Carrier

❶ Mast access unsafe

Extent: Hull specific

Effect:
Sailors climbing the mast are in potential danger due to lack of non-skid coating, insecure fall arrest staples, missing handgrabs, and sharp edges protruding into the mast access.

Resolution:
Plan to install additional fall arrest staples and improve security of existing staples, handgrabs installed, non-skid strips installed, and sharp edges shielded.

❷ Stores elevators inoperable

Extent: Hull specific

Effect:
Food and other supplies must be manually brought on board.

Resolution:
Elevators replaced with conveyors.

❸ Vacuum discharge system easily disabled

Extent: Hull specific

Effect:
While technically sound, the system is easily disabled by the introduction of inappropriate materials into the system, damage to the flushing button, or inadvertent disturbance during routine cleaning all of which can cause temporary system wide outages. Inoperability of this system affects toilets and urinals reducing quality of life on board the vessel.

Resolution:
Modifications to the system were made including adding a component to catch items that clog the system. Also, modifications were made to minimize system leaks on urinals. Research is also being done to improve the flushing buttons.

Source: GAO analysis of Navy data; U.S. Navy Photo by Mass Communication Specialist 2nd Class Mollie Rachel D. Majchrzak/Released

Figure 17: Selected Quality Issues on DDG 51 Class Ships

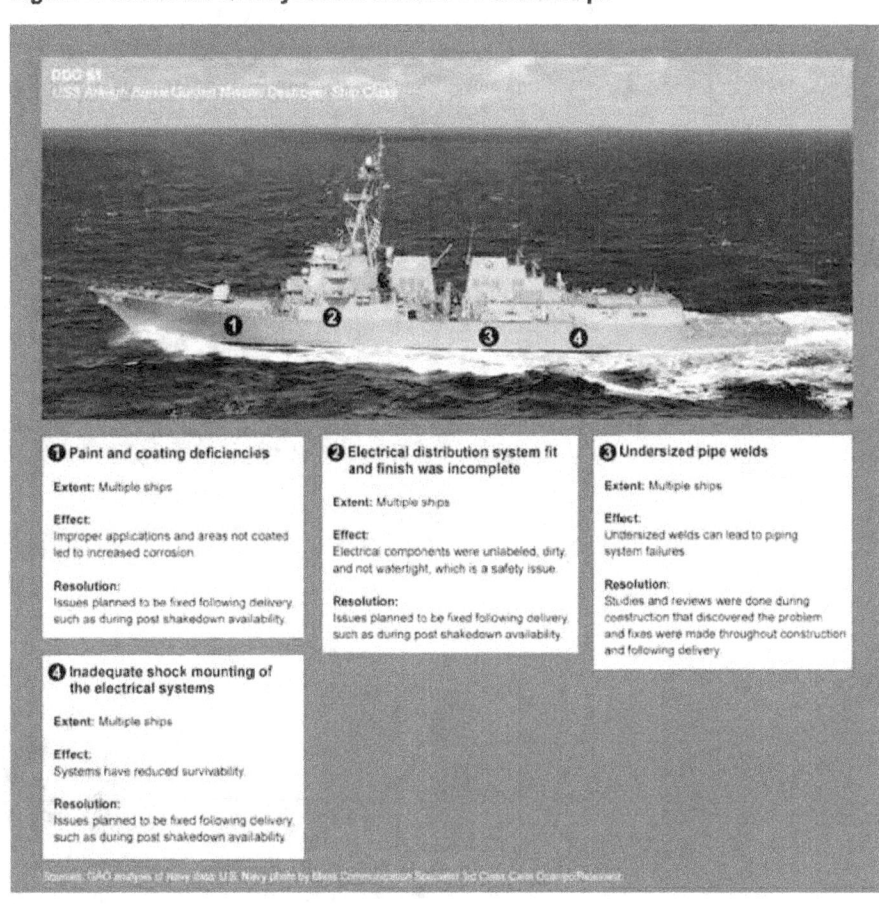

❶ Paint and coating deficiencies

Extent: Multiple ships

Effect:
Improper applications and areas not coated led to increased corrosion.

Resolution:
Issues planned to be fixed following delivery, such as during post shakedown availability.

❷ Electrical distribution system fit and finish was incomplete

Extent: Multiple ships

Effect:
Electrical components were unlabeled, dirty, and not watertight, which is a safety issue.

Resolution:
Issues planned to be fixed following delivery, such as during post shakedown availability.

❸ Undersized pipe welds

Extent: Multiple ships

Effect:
Undersized welds can lead to piping system failures.

Resolution:
Studies and reviews were done during construction that discovered the problem and fixes were made throughout construction and following delivery.

❹ Inadequate shock mounting of the electrical systems

Extent: Multiple ships

Effect:
Systems have reduced survivability.

Resolution:
Issues planned to be fixed following delivery, such as during post shakedown availability.

Sources: GAO analysis of Navy data; U.S. Navy photo by Mass Communication Specialist 3rd Class Carlos Ocampo/Released.

Figure 18: Selected Quality Issues on *USS Freedom* (LCS 1)

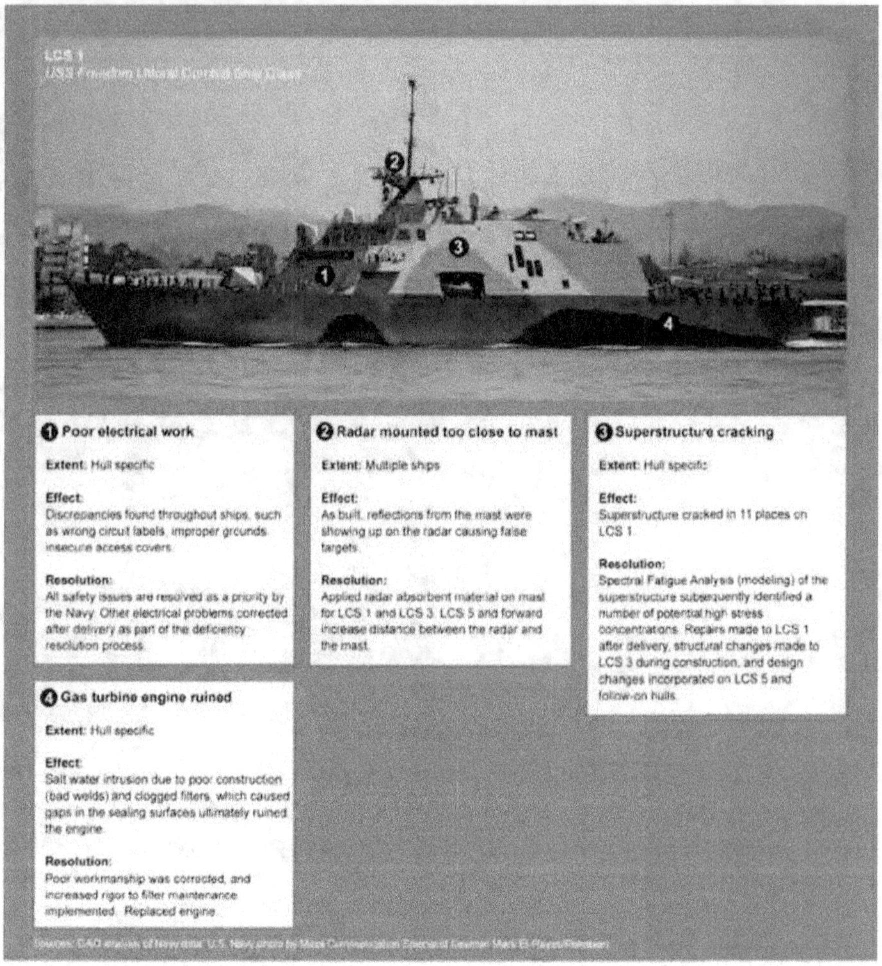

LCS 1
USS Freedom Littoral Combat Ship Class

❶ Poor electrical work

Extent: Hull specific

Effect:
Discrepancies found throughout ships, such as wrong circuit labels, improper grounds, insecure access covers.

Resolution:
All safety issues are resolved as a priority by the Navy. Other electrical problems corrected after delivery as part of the deficiency resolution process.

❷ Radar mounted too close to mast

Extent: Multiple ships

Effect:
As built, reflections from the mast were showing up on the radar causing false targets.

Resolution:
Applied radar absorbent material on mast for LCS 1 and LCS 3. LCS 5 and forward increase distance between the radar and the mast.

❸ Superstructure cracking

Extent: Hull specific

Effect:
Superstructure cracked in 11 places on LCS 1.

Resolution:
Spectral Fatigue Analysis (modeling) of the superstructure subsequently identified a number of potential high stress concentrations. Repairs made to LCS 1 after delivery, structural changes made to LCS 3 during construction, and design changes incorporated on LCS 5 and follow-on hulls.

❹ Gas turbine engine ruined

Extent: Hull specific

Effect:
Salt water intrusion due to poor construction (bad welds) and clogged filters, which caused gaps in the sealing surfaces ultimately ruined the engine.

Resolution:
Poor workmanship was corrected, and increased rigor to filter maintenance implemented. Replaced engine.

Sources: GAO analysis of Navy data; U.S. Navy photo by Mass Communication Specialist Seaman Mark El-Rayes/Released.

Figure 19: Selected Quality Issues on *USS Independence* (LCS 2)

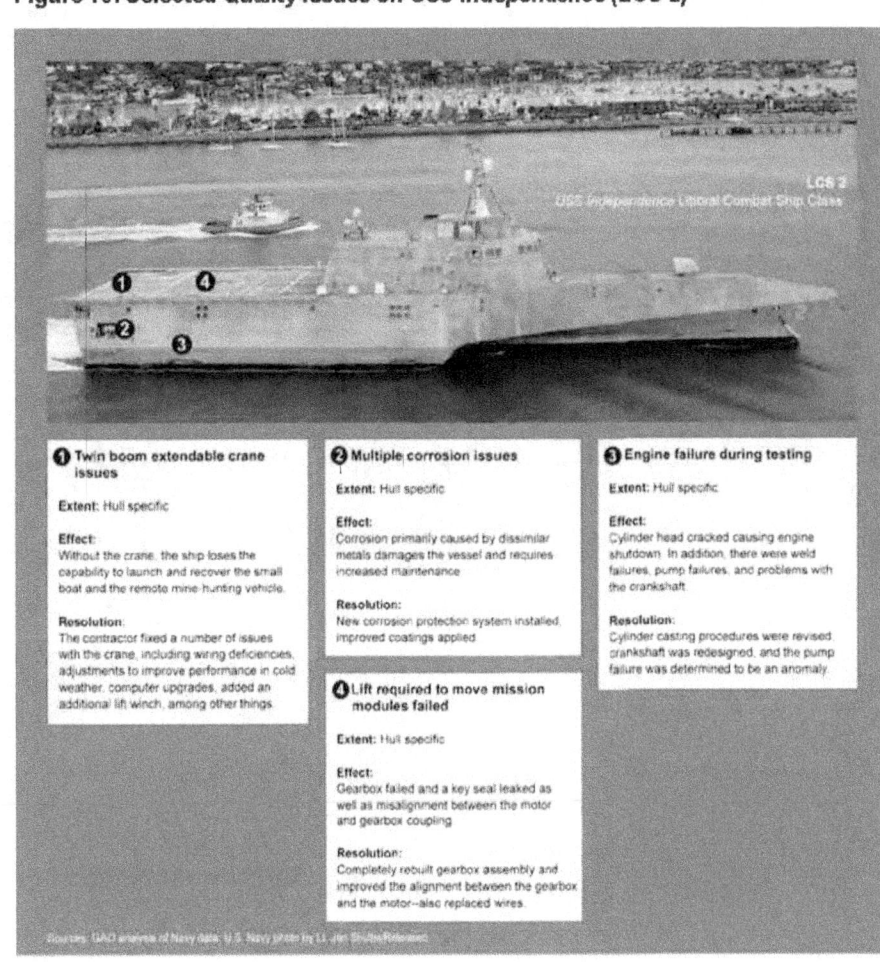

❶ Twin boom extendable crane issues

Extent: Hull specific

Effect:
Without the crane, the ship loses the capability to launch and recover the small boat and the remote mine-hunting vehicle.

Resolution:
The contractor fixed a number of issues with the crane, including wiring deficiencies, adjustments to improve performance in cold weather, computer upgrades, added an additional lift winch, among other things.

❷ Multiple corrosion issues

Extent: Hull specific

Effect:
Corrosion primarily caused by dissimilar metals damages the vessel and requires increased maintenance

Resolution:
New corrosion protection system installed, improved coatings applied

❹ Lift required to move mission modules failed

Extent: Hull specific

Effect:
Gearbox failed and a key seal leaked as well as misalignment between the motor and gearbox coupling

Resolution:
Completely rebuilt gearbox assembly and improved the alignment between the gearbox and the motor--also replaced wires.

❸ Engine failure during testing

Extent: Hull specific

Effect:
Cylinder head cracked causing engine shutdown. In addition, there were weld failures, pump failures, and problems with the crankshaft.

Resolution:
Cylinder casting procedures were revised, crankshaft was redesigned, and the pump failure was determined to be an anomaly.

Sources: GAO analysis of Navy data; U.S. Navy photo by Lt. Jan Shultis/Released.

Figure 20: Selected Quality Issues on *USS Makin Island* (LHD 8)

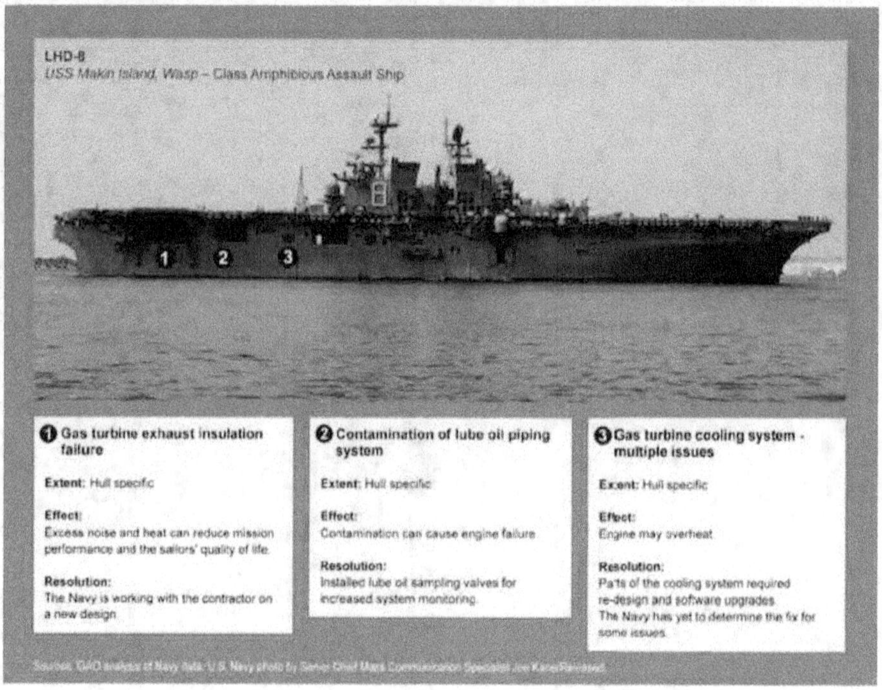

LHD-8
USS Makin Island, Wasp – Class Amphibious Assault Ship

❶ Gas turbine exhaust insulation failure

Extent: Hull specific

Effect:
Excess noise and heat can reduce mission performance and the sailors' quality of life.

Resolution:
The Navy is working with the contractor on a new design.

❷ Contamination of lube oil piping system

Extent: Hull specific

Effect:
Contamination can cause engine failure

Resolution:
Installed lube oil sampling valves for increased system monitoring.

❸ Gas turbine cooling system - multiple issues

Extent: Hull specific

Effect:
Engine may overheat.

Resolution:
Parts of the cooling system required re-design and software upgrades. The Navy has yet to determine the fix for some issues.

Sources: GAO analysis of Navy data; U.S. Navy photo by Senior Chief Mass Communication Specialist Joe Kane/Released.

Figure 21: Selected Quality Issues on LDP 17 Class Ships

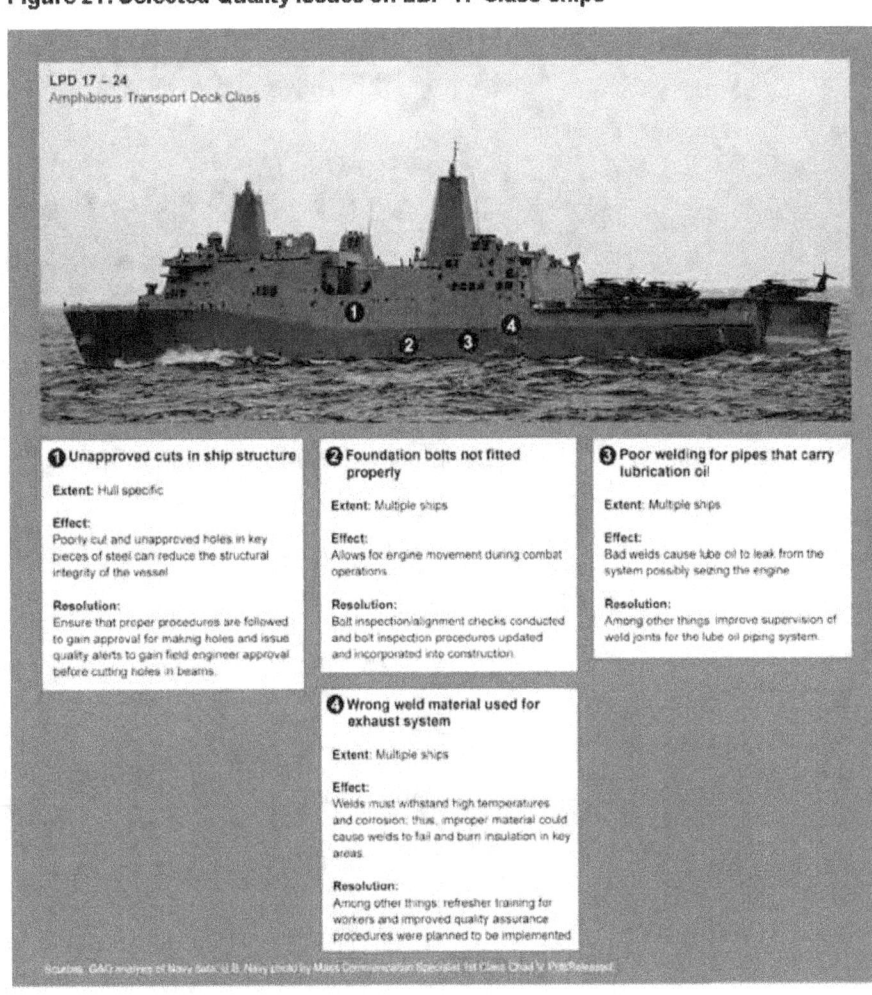

Source: GAO analysis of Navy data; U.S. Navy photo by Mass Communication Specialist 1st Class Chad V. Pritt/Released.

Figure 22: Selected Quality Issues on SSN 774 Class Submarines

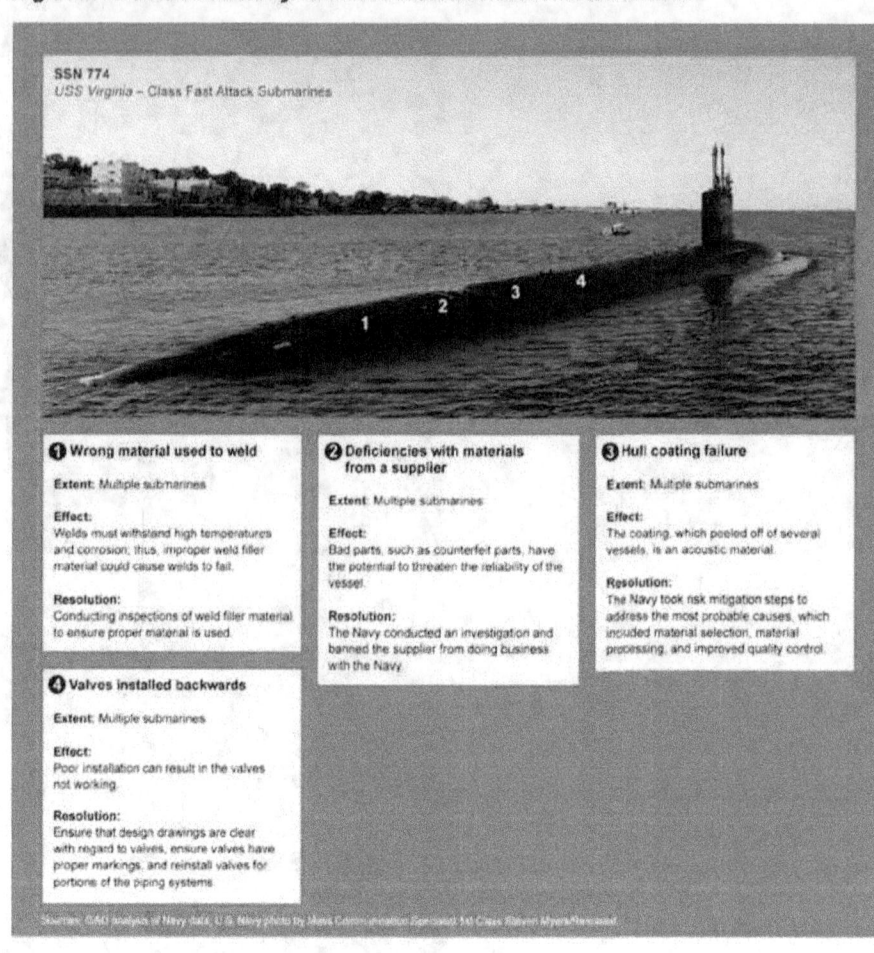

Figure 23: Selected Quality Issues on *USNS Howard O. Lorenzen* (T-AGM 25)

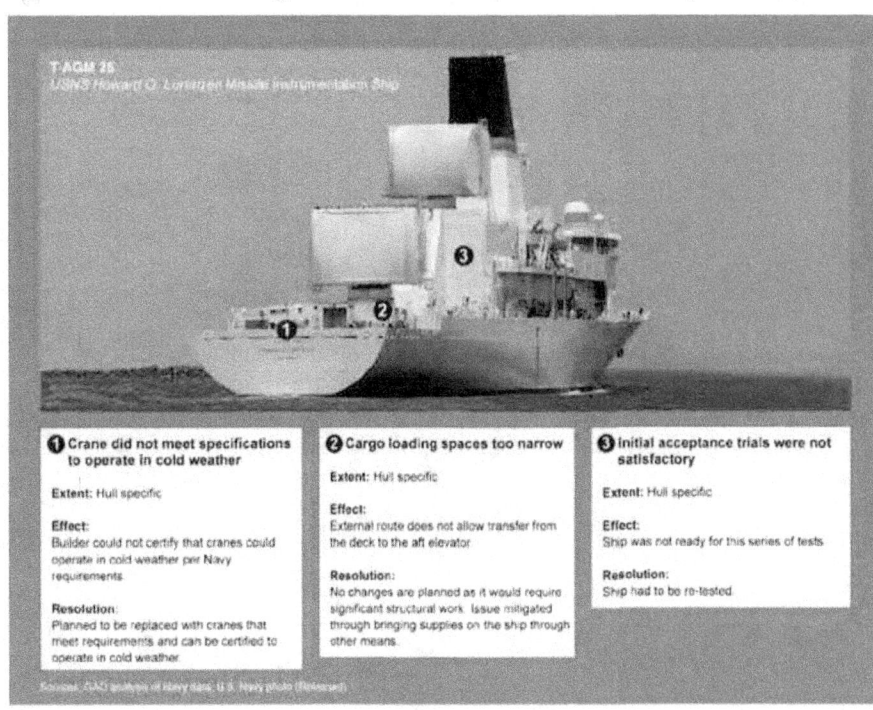

① **Crane did not meet specifications to operate in cold weather**

Extent: Hull specific

Effect:
Builder could not certify that cranes could operate in cold weather per Navy requirements.

Resolution:
Planned to be replaced with cranes that meet requirements and can be certified to operate in cold weather.

② **Cargo loading spaces too narrow**

Extent: Hull specific

Effect:
External route does not allow transfer from the deck to the aft elevator

Resolution:
No changes are planned as it would require significant structural work. Issue mitigated through bringing supplies on the ship through other means.

③ **Initial acceptance trials were not satisfactory**

Extent: Hull specific

Effect:
Ship was not ready for this series of tests.

Resolution:
Ship had to be re-tested.

Sources: GAO analysis of Navy data; U.S. Navy photo (Released)

Figure 24: Selected Quality Issues on T-AKE Class Ships

T-AKE
USNS Lewis and Clark Dry Cargo and Ammunition Ship Class

❶ Slow jet fuel delivery rate

Extent: Multiple ships

Effect:
Ship auxiliary pumps could only deliver jet fuel at a pace of 250 gallons per minute, far slower than the 3,000 gallons per minute rate of cargo fuel, thus inhibiting operations.

Resolution:
Redesign and modify system on T-AKE class vessels.

❷ Main engine couplings failed

Extent: Multiple ships

Effect:
The couplings, which connect the engine to the electricity generator, were improperly installed leading to safety risks and system breakdown.

Resolution:
Rebuilt all main diesel generator couplings on affected hulls—T-AKE 1, 4 and 9. And rebuilds planned for other vessels.

❸ Classwide main diesel engine issues

Extent: Multiple ships

Effect:
A multitude of issues including loose connections and damaged cables caused erroneous system shutdowns.

Resolution:
Actions required include: hand over hand cable inspections revising test procedures, and replaced certain parts.

❹ Crankshaft vibration damper failure

Extent: Multiple ships

Effect:
Significant damage to an engine on one ship occurred including damage to the cylinder, lube oil pumps, and engine block.

Resolution:
Replace all vibration damper fasteners on all T-AKE class vessels.

Sources: GAO analysis of Navy data; U.S. Navy photo by Mass Communication Specialist 3rd Class Bradley Evans/Released.

Appendix VIII: Characteristics of Select Commercial Ships and Offshore Structures

Each of the ship buyers we met with acquires large, expensive, and technologically advanced vessels. Below are illustrative examples of ships and offshore structures acquired by the firms we met with, and some of the key characteristics associated with each of the respective vessels.

Table 7: Key Characteristics of Selected Commercial Ships and Offshore Structures

Ship	Builder	Approximate cost (U.S. Dollars)	Length (feet)	Displacement (tons)	Notable characteristics
Celebrity Cruises, Inc. (subsidiary of Royal Caribbean Cruises, LTD.) *Reflection* – cruise ship (delivered October 2012)	Meyer Werft, Germany	$750 million	1,047 feet	61,609 tons displacement	The fifth and last ship of the *Solstice* ship class, completing a $3.7 billion shipbuilding program. The ship has a crew of 1,253, can accommodate 3,223 passengers, and incorporated advanced wastewater purification technology.
Chevron *Big Foot* – tension leg platform production facility (hull delivered March 2013; vessel completion estimated to be at end of 2013)	Daewoo Shipbuilding and Marine Engineering, Korea	$300 million (hull structure only)	373 feet	120,000 tons displacement	Upon completion, *Big Foot* will be the world's largest and deepest tension leg platform, with a capacity of 80,000 barrels of oil per day.
Ensco plc. DS-6 – drill ship (delivered January 2012)	Samsung Heavy Industries, Korea	$600 million	750 feet	105,822 tons displacement	Dynamically positioned drill ship can drill to 40,000 feet in up to 10,000 feet of water while maintaining a fixed, unanchored position.
Exxon Neftgas (a limited subsidiary of ExxonMobil) Sakhalin – 1 Project, Arkutun-Dagi Berkut Platform Topsides (estimated delivery June 2014)	Daewoo Shipbuilding and Marine Engineering, Korea	Proprietary information	Horizontal dimensions: 394 feet long by 230 feet wide Vertical dimensions: 328 feet from bottom of the deck to top of the drill rig	~40,000 tons displacement (topside unit only)	Upon completion in 2014, the topside will be transported and integrated to the offshore platform. The ice-resistant gravity based structure will become the largest oil and gas platform in Russia.
Noble Corporation *Noble Don Taylor* – drill ship (delivered April 2013)	Hyundai Heavy Industries, Korea	$600 million	752 feet	70,000 tons displacement	Dynamically positioned drill ship can drill to 40,000 feet in up to 10,000 feet of water while maintaining a fixed, unanchored position.
Norwegian Cruise Line, *Norwegian Gem* – cruise ship (delivered October 2007)	Meyer Werft, Germany	~$516 million	965 feet	50,259 tons displacement	The fourth ship in the *Jewel* ship class; has 1,188 cabins that can accommodate up to 2,384 passengers with a crew of 1,154.

Ship	Builder	Approximate cost (U.S. Dollars)	Length (feet)	Displacement (tons)	Notable characteristics
Qatar Petroleum and ExxonMobil Q-Max – Liquefied Natural Gas (LNG) Carrier (lead ship delivered June 2008)	(1) Daewoo Shipbuilding and Marine Engineering, Korea (2) Samsung Heavy Industries, Korea	$300 million	1,132 feet	179,000 tons displacement	Revolutionary size for an LNG carrier with novel reliquefaction technology and first to use a two-rudder and propeller design. Ship class built using three different hull and structure designs.
Royal Caribbean Cruises, LTD. *Oasis of the Sea* – cruise ship (delivered October 2009)	STX Finland Turku Shipyard, Finland	$1.4 billion	1,187 feet	116,00 tons displacement	The largest cruise ship in the world, with a crew of 2,100. The ship can accommodate 5,408 passengers at double occupancy and incorporated advanced wastewater purification technology.
Seadrill Ltd. *West Auriga* – drill ship (delivered April 2013)	Samsung Heavy Industries, Korea	$600 million	748 feet	107,474 tons displacement	Dynamically positioned drill ship can drill to 37,000 feet in up to 12,000 feet of water while maintaining a fixed, unanchored position.
Star Deep Water Petroleum, LTD (a Chevron-affiliated company) *Agbami* – Floating Production, Storage and Offloading vessel (delivered June 2008)	Daewoo Shipbuilding and Marine Engineering, Korea	$1.2 billion (hull only)	1,049 feet	460,000 tons displacement (full load)	At the time of delivery was the world's largest FPSO, with a production capacity of 250,000 barrels of oil and 25 million cubic feet of natural gas per day.

Source: Industry-provided data.

Appendix IX: Navy Shipbuilding Contract Types

In Navy shipbuilding, the type of contract used can significantly influence the final cost of the ship. Table 8 below illustrates the basic differences between fixed-price and cost-reimbursement contracts and how each contract type can incentivize quality.

Table 8: Common Navy Shipbuilding Contract Types and Associated Risks to Quality Goals

Type of contract	Contract type use and application	Navy responsibility	Shipbuilder responsibility	Who assumes the risk of cost overruns	How quality is affected
Cost-reimbursement contracts with incentive fee	Used when: Requirements not well-defined or lack of knowledge does not permit costs to be sufficiently estimated to use a fixed-price contract. Applications: Commonly used on lead ships.	Pays contractor's allowable costs incurred, to the extent prescribed by the contract. Ship buyer is not guaranteed a completed ship at the expected level of quality within cost or schedule estimates.	Shipbuilder makes good faith effort to meet ship buyer's needs within the estimated cost.	Navy	Incentive fee may allow shipbuilder to earn higher fee if costs are kept low (e.g., by minimizing rework).
Fixed-price-incentive (firm target) contract	Used when: A ceiling price, target cost, target profit and profit adjustment formula can be established that will provide a fair and reasonable incentive. Provides for the contractor to assume an appropriate share of the risk. Applications: Commonly used for follow-on ships in a class.	Navy pays fixed target price which includes shipbuilder's profit, but agrees to share cost overruns (or underruns) up to a ceiling price.	Shipbuilder delivers a ship at the expected level of quality, meeting all requirements and specifications as specified in the contract at or below the ceiling price.	Shared risk between Navy and shipbuilder up to agreed ceiling price. Shipbuilder generally bears most risk over that amount.	The Navy and the shipbuilder share cost overruns up to the agreed ceiling, which on previous contracts has been up to 138 percent of the target cost.

Type of contract	Contract type use and application	Navy responsibility	Shipbuilder responsibility	Who assumes the risk of cost overruns	How quality is affected
Firm-fixed-price contract	Used when: Fair and reasonable prices can be established at the outset. Applications: Limited use on new construction auxiliary and support ships.	Pays fixed price even if actual total cost of the ship falls short of or exceeds the contract price.	Shipbuilder delivers a ship at the expected level of quality, meeting all requirements and specifications as specified in the contract.	Shipbuilder	Contract type assigns risk to the shipbuilder and may provide direct incentive to ensure timely delivery of the ship at the expected level of quality. Additional incentives for shipbuilder to limit risks to quality, improve production efficiencies, and reduce costs.

Source: GAO analysis of information obtained from the Federal Acquisition Regulation, and the Department of Defense's Contract Pricing Preference Guide.

Appendix X: Comments from the Department of Defense

THE ASSISTANT SECRETARY OF DEFENSE
3015 DEFENSE PENTAGON
WASHINGTON, DC 20301-3015

ACQUISITION

091013

Ms. Michele Mackin
Director, Acquisition and Sourcing Management
U.S. Government Accountability Office
441 G Street, N.W.
Washington, DC 20548

Dear Ms. Mackin:

This is the Department of Defense response to the GAO Draft Report, GAO-13-527, "NAVY SHIPBUILDING: Opportunities Exist to Improve Practices Affecting Quality," dated August 2, 2013 (GAO Code 121032). The Department acknowledges receipt of the draft report.

As more fully explained in the enclosure, the Department concurs with recommendations 1 and 4 and partially concurs with recommendations 2, 3 and 5.

The Department appreciates the opportunity to comment on the draft report. For further questions concerning this report, please contact Mr. Jack Evans, Strategic and Tactical Systems/Deputy Director for Naval Warfare, 703-614-3170 or john.j.evans.civ@mail.mil.

Sincerely,

Katrina McFarland

Enclosure:
As stated

**GAO DRAFT REPORT DATED AUGUST 2, 2013
GAO-13-527 (GAO CODE 121032)**

**"NAVY SHIPBUILDING: OPPORTUNITIES EXIST TO
IMPROVE PRACTICES AFFECTING QUALITY"**

**DEPARTMENT OF DEFENSE COMMENTS
TO THE GAO RECOMMENDATIONS**

RECOMMENDATION 1: To improve the construction quality of ships delivered to the
Navy, GAO recommends that the Secretary of the Defense direct the Secretary of the
Navy to take the following action:

Ensure that the NAVSEA - level quality team provides support and a direct link to
directors of SUPSHIP quality assurance departments and is tasked with raising concerns
within NAVSEA about issues affecting or potentially affecting quality throughout the
acquisition process.

DoD RESPONSE: Concur – As stated in the report, NAVSEA is formulating plans to
reorganize the structure within the NAVSEA 04 Directorate to include the development
of a Quality Team that will provide a direct link to the directors of SUPSHIP QA
departments to enhance communication within NAVSEA about issues affecting or
potentially affecting quality throughout the acquisition process and as a resource for
identifying appropriate QA requirements for shipbuilding contracts. NAVSEA 08, Naval
Reactors, has responsibility of quality inspections of nuclear powered propulsion plants.
NAVSEA 08 also conducts periodic audits of both the nuclear-qualified shipyards' and
field activities' (to include SUPSHIP) performance and therefore receives direct input on
performance.

RECOMMENDATION 2: To improve the construction quality of ships delivered to the
Navy, GAO recommends that the Secretary of the Defense direct the Secretary of the
Navy to take the following action:

Clarify Navy policy (OPNAV Instruction 4700.8J) by clearly identifying at what point(s)
during the acquisition process contractor-responsible deficiencies are to be fully corrected
and ensure the policy is followed.

DoD RESPONSE: Partially Concur - OPNAV Instruction 4700.8J was updated in July
2012 with specific emphasis on ensuring the material status of the vessel is known at the
CNO level prior to preliminary acceptance of the vessel by the Navy. This instruction
requires that Acceptance Trials (AT) be conducted when all work including the
correction of significant deficiencies has been complete and provides for exceptions.
When, in special cases, it is desired to conduct AT with significant items incomplete, the
approval of the CNO shall be obtained by the Navy shipbuilding program manager prior
to presenting the ship to the INSURV President. Requests for this type of waiver will be
considered on a case-by-case basis. The instruction provides a similar process for the

2

preliminary acceptance of the ship to the Navy. Upon receipt of the INSURV AT report, the accepting authority shall request from the CNO, permission to accept delivery of the ship. If any waivers for delivery are required, they shall be requested in this message.

The instruction clearly states that waiver requests are to be minimized; however, in those extraordinary circumstances where it is considered in the best interest of the Navy to deviate from established requirements, waiver requests will be considered by the CNO. The instruction requires the waiver request specify the reason for non-correction of the deficiency or trial item, including estimated correction date if the waiver is granted. It requires the identification of available alternatives and the consequences of not granting the waiver and must identify any operational impact and risk associated with the waiver. It is also important to note that the delivery that is referred to in this section is "preliminary acceptance" by the government, and that 'final" acceptance by the government occurs at the end of the guarantee period which is typically one year following delivery and after completion of the final contract trials and closeout of all contractor deficiencies.

Consistent with this policy, the Navy will continue to strive to reduce the number of open deficiencies at the time of delivery to zero. As evidenced by the data in the report, the Navy has made noticeable improvements in the last several years. The policy as written reflects the goal of having no open significant deficiencies at the time of acceptance trials and no open deficiencies at the time of preliminary acceptance, while also reflecting the reality that it may be in the best interest to preliminarily accept the ship with open deficiencies and defines the process for ensuring CNO approval in such cases. One straight forward example of such a deficiency is with select amphibious ships which must depart a shipyard without select antennas in order to clear an overhead restriction. The policy provides for those occasions where exceptions are necessary and should be justified and approved on a case-by-case basis. However recognizing that OPNAV Instruction 4700.8 was recently revised and that the trend of fewer deficiencies at delivery needs to continue, the Navy will monitor the alignment between the stated goal and the actual material status at delivery to determine if future revisions to this instruction are warranted.

RECOMMENDATION 3: To improve the construction quality of ships delivered to the Navy, GAO recommends that the Secretary of the Defense direct the Secretary of the Navy to take the following action:

Provide guidance on the quality requirements in shipbuilding contracts, including the extent to which the SUPSHIP Management Group's Quality Performance Standard for Construction of Naval Vessels should be incorporated.

DoD RESPONSE: Partially Concur - The Federal Acquisition Regulation requires the inclusion of quality requirements in contracts, and recognize four general categories of requirements that can be used depending on the extent of quality assurance needed by the Government. Specifically, Federal Acquisition Regulation Subchapter G Part 46.0 (Quality Assurance) states that the Government shall ensure that contracts include

3

inspection and other quality requirements, including warranty clauses when appropriate, that are determined necessary to protect the government's interest. Contract requirements for quality will vary between shipbuilding contracts as a result of the type of acquisition, market conditions and level of technical risk and complexity. While the DoN program manager should encourage and support the contractor's efforts to assure quality, ultimately, the prime contractor is responsible to deliver a quality vessel. Therefore, from a DoD/DoN perspective, a key program success factor is selecting contractors that can demonstrate effective quality management. DoD guidance and support in accomplishing this objective is provided in the Defense Acquisition Guidebook Section 11.3.3.

NAVSEA's Contract Administration Quality Assurance Program (CAQAP) covers both hardware and technical data and is in accordance with DoD, DoN and NAVSEA policy. It includes provisions for tailoring the implementation of the program to the particular need, based on contractual requirements and specific programs being managed by the various SUPSHIP organizations. The CAQAP outlines requirements for a wide range of new construction, conversion, modernization, and major repair contracts assigned to a SUPSHIP. Elements of the SUPSHIP Management Group's Quality Performance Standard for Construction of Naval Vessels clearly have a place in select programs at specific SUPSHIP offices; however a blank incorporation into all shipbuilding contracts is not appropriate given the wide range (commercial research vessels to nuclear powered submarines) of shipbuilding programs that NAVSEA manages.

It is also noted that a noticeable decrease to open deficiencies at the time of delivery has occurred over the last several years and the quantity of all open deficiencies in very recent deliveries have been on the order of, or below the quantity of open deficiencies on the commercial projects listed in the report. However in an effort to continue the improvement in open deficiencies that exist at trials and delivery, the QA team discussed in recommendation #1 will be an available resource for consultation to the program manager and contracts who are responsible for determining the appropriate QA requirements for the shipbuilding contracts. The Department believes that the current progress and guidance on quality requirements along with the QA team discussed above are sufficient to continue the trend towards better quality products at an affordable price.

RECOMMENDATION 4: To improve the construction quality of ships delivered to the Navy, GAO recommends that the Secretary of the Defense direct the Secretary of the Navy to take the following action:

Provide guidance on use of payment withholds and retentions as a means to incentivize the shipbuilding contractor to promptly correct significant or persistent deficiencies and deliver a defect-free, or nearly defect free ship, to the Navy.

DoD RESPONSE: Concur – The Federal Acquisition Regulation Part 32 and the Navy's current contracting policies and operating procedures provide shipbuilding contract administration personnel the requisite flexibility, consistent with applicable law, regulation and contractual provisions, to withhold/retain progress payments, as necessary, in response to performance issues arising during ship construction. For example,

4

SECNAV Instruction 7810.12C contains guidance for payment and performance
retentions for shipbuilding contracts that provide for progress payments based on
percentage of completion basis. The Naval Sea Systems Command also provides
additional guidance for administration of shipbuilding contracts through the SUPSHIP
Operations Manual (SOM) (NAVSEA S0300-B2-MAN-010) and the NAVSEA
Contracts Handbook. The SOM Chapter 4 sets forth the financial management criteria
for the contract administration of NAVSEA shipbuilding contracts, including retentions.
Chapter 5 provides responsibilities for the SUPSHIP construction management team
including such things as the coordination, tracking, resolution and documentation of
guarantee deficiencies and all performance retentions. The NAVSEA Contracts
Handbook in Part 32 provides specific guidance for the administration of shipbuilding
progress payments and retentions.

As part of Better Buying Power (BBP) 2.0, the Department is taking several actions that
will assist in improving the construction quality of shipbuilding. BBP 2.0 focus area 3
has an initiative to better align contractor profitability with DoD goals through the use of
contract incentives. Also, in accordance with Section 804 (Department of Defense Policy
on Contractor Profits) of the National Defense Authorization Act for Fiscal Year 2013,
the Department is reviewing the profit guidelines in the DoD FAR Supplement to ensure
an appropriate link between contractor profit and performance. As part of these efforts,
OSD will revise and reissue guidance document on the use of incentives in defense
acquisition strategies. These new tools along with the existing tools provide sufficient
opportunity for program managers and contracting officers to ensure the construction of
quality ships for the Navy.

RECOMMENDATION 5: To improve the construction quality of ships delivered to the
Navy, GAO recommends that the Secretary of the Defense direct the Secretary of the
Navy to take the following action:

Assess the benefits and determine whether the following practices, in effect at some
SUPSHIP locations, would be useful in detecting quality problems across all locations:

- use of design drawings during SUPSHIP quality inspections, and
- increased focus on random and in-process inspections compared to use of
  resources for other types of inspections and observations.

DoD RESPONSE: Partially Concur - As noted in the report, the most cost effective
means of addressing quality issues is to drive the defect out of the process as opposed to
inspecting/correcting the defect after it has occurred. The use of design drawings during
the inspection and testing phase of a program is absolutely essential and is common
practice in Navy Ship acquisition programs. It is also noted that the use of checklists,
specifications and the statement of work are equally essential tools that may be used by
different personnel than those that inspect to drawings. The proper use of the proper
inspection tool by the appropriate personnel is occurring across the SUPSHIP
organization. The Department believes that random, work-in-process, and process-
oversight inspections are all necessary and appropriate and that the correct balance

5

among them must be continually assessed for each contract and shipbuilding location. One criteria or guidance will not fit all ship contracts and shipbuilders given the many different shipbuilding and repair programs within the Navy. The Department believes it is best left to the individual ship programs in consultation between SUPSHIP, the program manager, the technical community and contracts to establish the correct balance of inspection types.

Appendix XI: GAO Contact and Staff Acknowledgments

GAO Contact	Michele Mackin, (202) 512-4841 or mackinm@gao.gov.
Staff Acknowledgments	In addition to the contact above, Karen Zuckerstein, Assistant Director; Diana Moldafsky, Assistant Director; Christopher E. Kunitz; Peter W. Anderson; Ana I. Aviles; Mariana Calderon; Celina F. Davidson; Laurier R. Fish; Kristine Hassinger; Jean L. McSween; Jungjin Park, Roxanna T. Sun; Jeff M. Tessin; and Alyssa B. Weir made key contributions to this report.

GAO's Mission	The Government Accountability Office, the audit, evaluation, and investigative arm of Congress, exists to support Congress in meeting its constitutional responsibilities and to help improve the performance and accountability of the federal government for the American people. GAO examines the use of public funds; evaluates federal programs and policies; and provides analyses, recommendations, and other assistance to help Congress make informed oversight, policy, and funding decisions. GAO's commitment to good government is reflected in its core values of accountability, integrity, and reliability.
Obtaining Copies of GAO Reports and Testimony	The fastest and easiest way to obtain copies of GAO documents at no cost is through GAO's website (http://www.gao.gov). Each weekday afternoon, GAO posts on its website newly released reports, testimony, and correspondence. To have GAO e-mail you a list of newly posted products, go to http://www.gao.gov and select "E-mail Updates."
Order by Phone	The price of each GAO publication reflects GAO's actual cost of production and distribution and depends on the number of pages in the publication and whether the publication is printed in color or black and white. Pricing and ordering information is posted on GAO's website, http://www.gao.gov/ordering.htm.
	Place orders by calling (202) 512-6000, toll free (866) 801-7077, or TDD (202) 512-2537.
	Orders may be paid for using American Express, Discover Card, MasterCard, Visa, check, or money order. Call for additional information.
Connect with GAO	Connect with GAO on Facebook, Flickr, Twitter, and YouTube. Subscribe to our RSS Feeds or E-mail Updates. Listen to our Podcasts. Visit GAO on the web at www.gao.gov.
To Report Fraud, Waste, and Abuse in Federal Programs	Contact: Website: http://www.gao.gov/fraudnet/fraudnet.htm E-mail: fraudnet@gao.gov Automated answering system: (800) 424-5454 or (202) 512-7470
Congressional Relations	Katherine Siggerud, Managing Director, siggerudk@gao.gov, (202) 512-4400, U.S. Government Accountability Office, 441 G Street NW, Room 7125, Washington, DC 20548
Public Affairs	Chuck Young, Managing Director, youngc1@gao.gov, (202) 512-4800 U.S. Government Accountability Office, 441 G Street NW, Room 7149 Washington, DC 20548

Please Print on Recycled Paper.